AN
ATTITUDE OF
EXCELLENCE!

HOW THE **BEST** ORGANIZATIONS
GET THE **BEST** PERFORMANCE
FROM THE **BEST** PEOPLE

WILLIE JOLLEY

JOLLEY PUBLISHING

Published by Jolley Publishing, LLC,
a division of Willie Jolley Worldwide, Inc., Washington, D.C.
Jolley Publishing, LLC
P.O. Box 55459
Washington, D.C. 20040
www.jolleypublishing.com

Willie Jolley books are available at special discounts for bulk purchases. Plus special editions, personalized covers or covers with corporate branding and logos can be specially printed to meet the needs of our clients. For more information on bulk sales or special orders contact 202-723-8863 or email info@williejolley.com.

Design and composition by Greenleaf Book Group LLC
Cover design by Greenleaf Book Group LLC
Cover photo by Jim Johnson Photography/PictureStoryStudio.com

Publisher's Cataloging-in-Publication Data
(Prepared by The Donohue Group, Inc.)

Jolley, Willie.
   An attitude of excellence : how the best organizations get the best performance from the best people / Willie Jolley. -- 1st ed.
      p. ; cm.
   ISBN: 978-0-9841049-0-1
1. Employee motivation. 2. Corporate culture. 3. Success in business. 4. Career development. 5. Employee morale. 6. Employees--Attitudes. I. Title.
HF5549.5.M63 J65 2009
658.3/14   2009906131

Part of the Tree Neutral™ program, which offsets the number of trees consumed in the production and printing of this book by taking proactive steps, such as planting trees in direct proportion to the number of trees used: www.treeneutral.com

Printed in the United States of America on acid-free paper

12 13 14 15 16   10 9 8 7 6 5 4 3

First Edition

CONTENTS

"Talk about a brilliant, inspiring, motivating book! Reading it—laced with powerful, practical examples—affirms and empowers you to *choose* success, to *choose* excellence, to see change and constant improvement as an ally instead of a fearsome enemy, to *choose* a complementary team style where strengths are made productive and weakness made irrelevant because of the strengths of other team members. Intertwining personal and organizational/cultural development is so vital and beautifully illustrated throughout.

What an illuminating, uplifting read! I can 'hear' and 'feel' Willie entertaining as well as educating."

—Stephen R. Covey, author of *The 7 Habits of Highly Effective People* and *The 8th Habit: From Effectiveness to Greatness*

INTRODUCTION

Excellence can be attained if you
Care more than others think is wise,
Risk more than others think is safe,
Dream more than others think is practical,
And expect more than others think is possible!
—Anonymous

*Finally, beloved, whatever is true, whatever is honorable, whatever is just, whatever is pure, whatever is pleasing, whatever is commendable, if there is **any excellence** and if there is anything worthy of praise, think about these things.*
—Philippians 4:8 (Revised Standard Version)

An "Attitude of Excellence"—this concept captivated me from the very first moment I wrote it on my idea pad. The more I looked at this simple combination of words, the more I was struck by the fact that this concept combines two words that are widely used individually to express behaviors that many of us say we want to pursue but do not really pursue with vigor. We often talk about how "attitude determines altitude," yet most of us do very little to actually grow our "attitude muscle." Likewise, we hear people talk about excellence, yet it is a quality that often evades us.

This book is written to help you develop a new framework for achieving excellence; a new way of building your attitude muscle; and a new way of creating a culture of excellence for your organization by developing a new attitude for yourself: An Attitude of Excellence!

An Attitude of Excellence has two major objectives:

1. To help organizations create a culture of excellence that enhances their performance and profits.

2. To help individuals achieve greater personal success, both at work and at home.

The book has two distinct parts; in fact, it is like having two books combined into one. Part 1, "The Will to Win: Developing a Culture of Excellence," is an organizational development guide, which focuses on the steps necessary to create a culture of excellence. I concentrate in these chapters on the areas that can help an organization excel and improve performance, productivity, and profits.

Part 2, "Personal Development: Five Simple Steps to Five-Star Success," focuses on the components that make the individual within a company a more powerful part of a winning team. If the people who work in any organization can become better individually and can express that improvement in their day-to-day activities, then that organization can start to see rapid improvement because of the power of synergy and momentum. In these chapters I share secrets I have learned while working around the world with such leading-edge organizations as Microsoft, Wal-Mart, Marriott, Cox, Dell, Verizon Communications, and Prudential Insurance of Australia. The secrets are designed as "simple steps" that can quickly be implemented in both your professional and your personal life.

This book gives people within organizations a new perspective on the impact that individuals can have on the long-term success of an organization. It will help people in today's workforce position themselves for long-term employment even in these changing and challenging times! And it will help organizations not just survive but also thrive during tough economic times. My goal is for you to prosper and do more in the future than you've done in the past. In short, I want to help you create a more fulfilling future while making more money, starting right now!

So let's get going in our quest for an Attitude of Excellence!

THE WILL TO WIN: DEVELOPING A CULTURE OF EXCELLENCE

1

THE PATH TO EXCELLENCE

If a man is called to be a street sweeper, he should sweep streets even as Michelangelo painted, or Beethoven composed music, or Shakespeare wrote poetry. He should sweep streets so well that all the hosts of heaven and earth will pause to say, "Here lived a great street sweeper who did his job well!"

—Martin Luther King Jr.

Excellence is a word used frequently, but its quality is rarely attained. *Webster's* dictionary defines *excellence* as "that which is of the best and finest quality; that which is superior, outstanding, and first class." It is going the extra mile and going beyond the call of duty. Therefore, excellence is a quality that is to be modeled. I contend that excellence is not only a quality but also an attitude! It is an attitude that makes you want to do more, to be more, and to achieve more!

Aristotle said: "We are what we repeatedly do. Excellence, then, is not an act, but a habit." I want to help you make excellence a habit rather than a once in a while occurrence.

DEVELOPING A CULTURE OF EXCELLENCE: CREATING A FIVE-STAR ORGANIZATION

Have you ever been to a five-star resort, a five-star hotel, or a five-star restaurant? If so, how did it make you feel? Did it make you feel good? Did it make you feel special? Did it make you feel important? Did you want to go back again? Did you wonder about the types of people who could afford that lifestyle and how it would feel to always live that kind of life? That is the nature of the five-star success system, and that is what this book is all about.

To achieve five-star success is to operate in an environment of excellence; we go to five-star resorts, hotels, and restaurants because they are the best of the best. I have discovered five secrets that can lead to five-star success in your business or organization as well as in your personal life. Although I touch on them here, I will give you great detail about each of these powerful secrets a little later in the book. So keep reading and get ready, get ready, get ready!

Attitude of Excellence Secret #1:
Dynamic Leadership Development

Create leaders at every level of the organization. Five-star organizations recognize the power of developing leaders at every level and empowering employees to do whatever is necessary to serve their customers. Great organizations recognize that before you can lead many, you must be able to lead one—yourself!

Attitude of Excellence Secret #2:
Proactive Change Management

Recognize that change is an ally, not the enemy, and develop skills for managing change. If you embrace the components of change, challenge, and choices, you can learn to succeed as you "GROW," not just "GO," through the changes.

Attitude of Excellence Secret #3:
Dedicated Teamwork

Embrace the incredible power of teamwork. Those who think like a team and work like a team are those who win like a team! Keep in mind that great teams care for each other, cover for each other, and encourage each other. Everyone is an MVP—a most valuable and valued player—because the chain is only as strong as the weakest link.

Attitude of Excellence Secret #4:
Wow Customer Service

Wow the customer with amazing customer service and your business will grow! As you grow your people, you will grow their capacity to serve, and great people tend to give great service. Remember that the greatest leaders are always the greatest servants.

Attitude of Excellence Secret #5:
World-Class Attitude Enhancement

> Develop a positive attitude and a positive outlook, in-look, and up-look! Learn to see that change is good when your attitude is great! When it's all said and done, it's *all* about your attitude!

THE POWER OF ATTITUDE, APTITUDE, AND APPETITE

Let me ask you a couple of questions: "Do you want to win? Do you *really* want to win?" I ask these questions at the beginning of my presentations, and I always get the same response: "Yes, I really want to win!" While I believe most people do want to win, the definitive questions then become: "How badly do you want to win? Are you willing to do what is uncomfortable? Are you willing to stretch? Are you willing to do some things differently and to do some different things? Are you willing to change in order to win?" The concept of truly wanting to win is one of the main premises to begin with as you create an Attitude of Excellence.

Bill Russell, former all-star center for the Boston Celtics, is an example of someone who learned the secrets to winning and made his team better by helping them learn to win as well. He was a five-time winner of the National Basketball Association Most Valuable Player award and a twelve-time All-Star. He created a culture of excellence whenever and wherever he played. He went from winning a championship his final year in college to leading the Celtics to eleven championships in thirteen years—the most championships won by any team in NBA history!

What is most amazing about Bill Russell was not that he was a prolific scorer but that he was a player who focused his energy on creating a winning culture. Russell said he was not about scoring, he was about winning! In his book, *Russell Rules* (NAL Trade, 2002), he wrote: "Everyone can win, but it takes teamwork. Then you must add three key ingredients . . . Attitude, Aptitude, and Appetite!"

So in order to win, you too must have a *winner's* attitude, aptitude, and appetite! In other words, you must have an Attitude of Excellence about you and your team!

DO YOU WANT MORE IN THE FUTURE?

Do you want more in the future than you've had in the past? Do you want to *be* more in the future than you've been in the past? Would you like to make more money in the future than you've made in the past? If you answered "yes" to these questions, then please continue to read on. If you answered "no," you need to read on anyway! I am sure you will get a new insight in the next few pages that will change your thinking for a lifetime!

In a time of endless competition, nanosecond change, and economic uncertainty, it is critical to look to the long term and recognize that excellence is essential to greater personal and professional success. While many people speak of the importance of "branding," which is a popular concept used to discuss how people should position themselves in the minds of others, it is essential to create a personal brand of excellence.

To increase our income, it is important to focus on the power of creating a reputation for excellence. The brand, or reputation, for excellence is one of the secrets of those who succeed in life and business. Developing a reputation for excellence is a way to build our personal brands and increase our personal wealth!

History offers us many examples of people and organizations that had quick success and made money in the short term but could not sustain that success. More often than not they failed to sustain their success because they did not make a commitment to excellence. They were willing to take shortcuts, and some of those shortcuts proved to be their undoing! Developing a reputation, for excellence is the best insurance for long-term wealth and success.

Over the last few years we have heard story after story of downsizing, rightsizing, reengineering, and restructuring. Many such stories involve people who were close to retirement after years of dedicated service to a company, but due to circumstances beyond their control, they lost their jobs.

In today's rapidly changing job market, we must pursue excellence on a daily basis for there is no job security! Virtually no one can guarantee they will stay employed or stay in good standing in their present position. There could be a sudden change in the direction of the company or the industry or the economy that affects your job security. Numerous scenarios, beyond your control, could impact your present employment. But you will greatly enhance your job security by developing a reputation for excellence! Employers are always looking for talented individuals with a desire or hunger to learn. They are always looking and waiting for excellent people to become available. While there is no such thing as job security, excellence is the best remedy for a changing and challenging marketplace.

I didn't grasp the full significance of this phenomenon until I was older and saw examples of people who always seemed to be in demand, even when others were losing their jobs. A friend who had worked at the same company for a number of years was concerned about her job prospects when the owner of the company decided to retire and close the business. She thought she would have a difficult time finding another job since she was older and most of the workforce in her industry was so much younger. Yet, as soon as the word got out that her company was closing, she was bombarded with offers—from companies who knew of her reputation for excellence and wanted to have her on their team!

This can be seen in other areas too, especially the sports industry. Imagine, for example, that after winning numerous championships in basketball over recent years, the Los Angeles Lakers were bought by a new ownership group. And imagine that the new owners decided they wanted to start over with their own group of players and coaches, so they fired the coach, Phil Jackson, and the star player, Kobe Bryant. How long do you think it would take for Coach Jackson and perennial All-Star Bryant to get new jobs? About a nanosecond! Why? Because they both have developed reputations for excellence.

Today, there are excellent workers who, through no fault of their own, have lost their jobs because of economic conditions. Companies that were once market leaders, like Woolworth's department stores, or Lehman Brothers, lost market share and laid off workers or closed up shop completely. Without question, the workers who had developed a reputation for excellence were always the first to get hired by other companies. Why? Employers are always looking for great talent and seeking people who have a reputation for excellence.

The secret, though, is to develop a reputation for excellence before you need it! As the old saying goes, "It is always best to dig your well before you are thirsty!"

THE POWER OF A REPUTATION OF EXCELLENCE

My childhood friend Biddy and I started college together at American University in Washington, D.C. During her sophomore year, Biddy got married, left school, and started working in the federal government as an entry-level employee. Her job was to answer phones and to make photocopies of policy manuals. Yet she did her job with such zeal that she quickly became a hit in the office. She would answer the phones by saying, "It's a great day! How can I serve you?" And she did that from nine o'clock in the morning until five o'clock in the evening. She would even answer the phone with that same enthusiasm after hours while she waited for her husband, Dexter, to pick her up. She often worked an extra hour every day, never looking at the clock and always focusing on what needed to be done!

When she was asked to make photocopies, she would make them with such precision that many people in the office thought they had been sent out to a printing company. When she made copies of the training manuals, Biddy made an extra one that she could read at night so she could create a list of suggested improvements to share with her supervisor. Biddy would always say: "If these make sense to you, please feel free to use them. If not, just throw them in the trash." Even though she enjoyed her job, she often talked about going back to college and finishing her degree as soon as she and her husband could get their finances straightened out.

Biddy quickly moved from an entry-level position (GS-2) to that of an administrator (GS-7) before she became pregnant with her first child. When she returned from maternity leave, she showed the same spirit of excellence. She still answered the phones with enthusiasm, even after hours. She still made photocopies with a precision that astounded the staff, continuing to make one for herself and jotting down ideas that she thought might be helpful for the team. She moved from a GS-7 up to a GS-9, and then she became pregnant again.

This time, however, the cost of placing two children in childcare was more than Biddy brought in! Dexter told her it would be more cost-effective if she stayed home. She did, for a few years, but once the kids were school-age, Biddy started looking into going back to work. A federal government job freeze proved a challenge, and the only job that was available was at an entry level (GS-2), answering phones and making photocopies of the policy manuals, where she had begun years earlier! Needless to say, Biddy took the job and went back to work with the same enthusiasm and the same work ethic as before.

One day when she answered the phone, the person on the other end was someone she had not heard from in many years. It was her very first supervisor, and he had been trying to find her! He spoke of how he had never forgotten the impact of her positive attitude. He had raved to others over the years about her Attitude of Excellence and that her positive attitude had become a model he shared with new employees. He explained he was now the director of a new agency and he was looking for a special assistant. He wondered if she would be willing to leave her present job to come work with him. Of course, that would entail a raise that was outside the dimensions of the freeze. Plus, she would have a staff of people she would supervise! She giggled and said, "Excuse me, sir, . . . when do I start?"

She took the job and was excellent in the position, continuing to go the extra mile. When others didn't quickly answer the phone, she would with her characteristic: "It's a great day! How can I serve you?"

Today, Biddy continues to show that excellence truly is the best job security and job advancement strategy. She is now the director of policy and programs for the Department of Energy and continues to pursue excellence with a passion! And, she literally gets job offers every week. Recently, I spoke at a government agency where she used to work. When I mentioned I knew her, the staff raved about how she had been such a bright

light and how her enthusiasm for excellence had been contagious throughout their organization. They all talked about her
Attitude of Excellence!

And by the way, when her first child graduated from college, so did Biddy—on the same day. Biddy had found a way
to go back to college while working and raising her children.
When I asked Biddy the secret to her success, she told me, "I
learned that excellence offers no excuses but rather focuses on
getting the job done, even in the midst of challenging situations. There is no substitute for excellence," she went on. "It is
the best job security!"

2

SECRET 1 — DYNAMIC LEADERSHIP DEVELOPMENT

Create leaders at every level of the organization. Five-star organizations recognize the power of developing leaders at every level and empowering employees to do whatever is necessary to serve their customers. Great organizations recognize that before you can lead many, you must be able to lead one—yourself!

Why is it that some organizations consistently stand head and shoulders above their competition? How is it that some organizations reach five-star status while others are never able to grasp the golden ring? The second-tier companies and organizations often work very hard, but five-star success eludes them. I was intrigued by that dilemma, so I set out to find the answer.

I sought out organizations with five-star ratings and interviewed their top people, and I found that all of the companies had similar environments. They had developed a culture that inspired an Attitude of Excellence. And, because I receive invitations to speak at top organizations around the world, I have been able to observe, investigate, and collect information about the principles that separate outstanding companies from their lesser competitors.

The pursuit of excellence was a consistent guiding principle in both the professional and the personal lives of personnel of these successful organizations. This leads me to my first point, which is often overlooked in attaining success: the best companies always commit to getting the best people and developing them into great leaders at every level of the organization! Great sports teams are always trying to hire, acquire, and field the best players. And the same is true for great businesses. They know that great people are the secret to creating outstanding organizations.

HIRE, ACQUIRE, OR DEVELOP

I was asked to be the closing speaker for a recent Dell Computer international leadership conference. I went a day early so I could listen to some of the other presenters they had invited. (They had some real heavy hitters I wanted to hear.) The night before my speech, I had dinner with the program director. I mentioned to him that I was amazed at the program they had put together and honored to be in the mix of speakers. I did have one question for him, though. I was intrigued as to why Dell would spend such a great amount of money on this meeting. I wondered why they would make such a major investment for such a small group of people, only three hundred or so of their top managers.

In response, he shared a powerful tenet on success: "We want to be the best at what we do in the world. We want to lead the field, and in order to be the best, we must have the best people. And if we cannot *hire* them, we will *make* them!"

All I could say in reply was, "Wow!" It was a real "aha" moment for me because it brought to the surface one of the best-kept secrets of supersuccessful companies. Five-star companies always start with five-star people, and they are constantly working to hire, acquire, or develop them. If they cannot hire them, they will take good raw materials and make them into diamonds. The secret is that successful companies are making a commitment to get the best people in order to achieve the best results!

Leading-edge companies consistently invest in the growth and development of their workforce. They know that in order to grow your profits, you must first grow your people. The best way to grow your future is to grow yourself, and the best way to grow your organization is to grow your people! Leading- edge organizations are committed to developing people because they understand that there is a direct correlation between the success of their employees and the success of the organization.

THE IMPACT THAT ENCOURAGEMENT HAS ON PROFITS

In preparing for a program for the Society of Human Resource Managers, I had the opportunity to interview a number of top-notch HR directors from around the world. I asked each of them, "What are the secrets to your creating happy and productive employees?" The information I received in answer to that question was priceless.

They told me that the more employees are encouraged to do their best, the more their morale went up and their productivity went up. As employees are empowered to communicate honestly and openly, their performance improves. Also, those companies that find or develop good talent are more often willing to work with valued employees to keep them engaged, even if the employees' lives change and they have to relocate to other cities. Many companies were looking at ways to engage new technologies to keep the employees on the team. One manager put it this way: "Everyone has bumps in life. If you are able to unshackle your mind and think bigger and think differently, you are able to open up incredible possibilities for productivity and for growth of the company and the person." Many of the managers said they were able to create ways to keep good people on their teams, even if those people moved to different cities.

In addition, organizations that are willing to think differently and act differently can create employees who become their best marketing vehicles for adding great new talent to their organizations! Happy and excited team members are more apt to tell their friends and therefore to become magnets for attracting top-quality people to join the company. To get the best people you must be willing to think differently and empower them to do the same.

Southwest Airlines is one great example of this type of different thinking. They believe their people are their greatest asset. Southwest sees their employees as their first priority. They call it an "employee-first customer service model that focuses on the fact that happy employees tend to serve customers with greater happiness." Herb Kelleher, the founder of Southwest Airlines, said in an interview:

> Anyone can buy a plane, but our people make this airline a success. It's more than providing the customer a value. It is giving them an experience. I want our customers to leave with a smile on their face and communicate that smile to everyone they talk to that day. This is the secret . . . because our competitors can all buy airplanes; it is the experience that our associates give the customers that is the hardest thing for our competitors to imitate. (Spirit Magazine, June 2009)

The freedom to serve the customers and have fun in the process is why Southwest can get their associates to sing, tell jokes, and even climb up in the overhead bin and say, "Surprise!" when it's opened. It is the people who create the organization.

Marriott Hotels and Resorts and the Ritz, Carlton continue to increase their market share by improving the lives of the people who work there. They know that happy, excited associates tend to share that happiness and excitement with customers, and thereby tend to give better service. These two luxury accommodations giants take surveys every few months: one to determine customer satisfaction levels and another to determine associate (employee) satisfaction levels. (By the way, Marriott and Ritz-Carlton employees are not called "employees"; rather, they are called "associates" because they are partners in making each hotel a success.)

MAKE IT CONTAGIOUS—CATCH THE EXCELLENCE ATTITUDE

Excellence is making a commitment to do the right thing, at the right time, in the right way; to do some things better than they were ever done before; to eliminate errors; to know both sides of the question; to be courteous; to be an example; to work for the love of work; to anticipate requirements; to develop resources; to recognize no impediments; to master circumstances; to act from reason rather than rule; to be satisfied with nothing short of our very best!
—*Marshall Field & Company*

We must "Catch the Excellence Attitude" if we expect to create a culture of excellence! It is essential to start with knowing the vision of the organization. It is quite possible to achieve goals that others consider impossible when employees grab the vision of the company and pursue it with an Attitude of Excellence.

But in order for the team to catch the vision, someone must first sell the vision! And before you can sell the vision to others, you must first sell the vision to yourself.

Leading-edge organizations have very clear visions of where they are going; they share and articulate that vision to their entire company; and then they sell their people on it—with excitement and enthusiasm! Leading-edge organizations make the commitment to make the vision a reality. And once they start the quest for excellence, they take the next step, which is making a daily commitment to their commitment! In time, it becomes an attitude . . . an Attitude of Excellence!

When we think of a person having "an attitude," we generally think of someone with a bad or negative disposition. I believe that attitude is viral in nature and can be transmitted from one person to another! Just as a person with a negative attitude can infect an organization and make it an unpleasant place to work, a person with a positive attitude—an Attitude of Excellence—can lift the spirit and climate of an organization and help foster an environment where people are excited about work and are encouraged to let their new ideas flow freely! The challenge is this: people who are negative readily share their thoughts with others, while people with positive attitudes often tend to keep their thoughts to themselves or express those thoughts only to their close friends.

The quality of a person's life is in direct proportion to their commitment to excellence, regardless of their chosen field of endeavor.
—*Vince Lombardi*

Vince Lombardi is an example of a person with a positive attitude and a positive outlook who was able to change the destiny of an organization with his Attitude of Excellence!

In a special Super Bowl edition of *Parade* magazine in recent memory, Jeremy Schaap wrote an article about Super Bowl history, emphasizing how Vince Lombardi changed a losing group of football players in Green Bay, Wisconsin, into a team that became legendary. The article shared some comments from Bart Starr, the quarterback of the team, which had won only one game the previous season! Starr describes the first time he met Vince Lombardi. It was at the first team meeting with the new coach, and Vince Lombardi told the players: "Gentlemen, I want you to know that we are going to relentlessly chase perfection, knowing full well we will not catch it, because nothing is perfect. But we are going to relentlessly chase it, because in the process we will cross a street called excellence, and in doing that we will catch excellence!" They did, in fact, create and catch excellence and went on to win five league championships and the first two Super Bowls.

Starr remembers that after that first meeting with Lombardi, he ran to a phone and called his wife and told her something was different—something had changed! He believed that the team was going to win, and win big, because the new coach had convinced him they could, and would, be excellent!

Starr was later inducted into the Football Hall of Fame and he became a very successful businessman and philanthropist. He said that Lombardi taught him that when you "catch excellence"—the *attitude* of excellence—then you will be transformed and amazed at what you will accomplish, not just at work but in every part of your life.

At a later date, while I was waiting at a gate for my departing flight, I noticed a gentleman wearing a Green Bay Packers sweater. I recognized him from television and realized it was Paul Hornung, the star running back of the Green Bay Packers for seven of Lombardi's eight years as coach of the team. I asked Hornung if the stories about how Vince Lombardi helped the team catch the Attitude of Excellence were true or just urban myths. Without hesitation, he said, "Yes! Those are not myths. They're true stories! He instilled an Attitude of Excellence and that was the reason why we won!"

SUCCESS AND EXCELLENCE ARE CHOICES

The fame that goes with wealth and beauty is fleeting and fragile; intellectual superiority [an Attitude of Excellence] is a possession glorious and eternal.
—*Sallust*

In every success manual and in every success study, it is consistently stated that success is a choice, not a chance. In order to effectively achieve the success you dream about, you must first choose to succeed. It is the same for those who want to create a life of excellence: you must make the choice; you must decide.

In my book *A Setback Is a Setup for a Comeback*, I shared something about choice that elicited an incredible response from readers around the world. "Successful people choose to be successful! Successful people make a choice—a conscious decision—to succeed. They understand that decision and choice are integral parts of the success formula. Success is not a chance but rather a choice!"

Rick Pitino, former coach of the Boston Celtics and the 1996 NCAA champions, the Kentucky Wildcats, wrote in *Success Is A Choice* (Broadway, 1998) that success will not "happen unless you choose to make it happen. Success is not a lucky break. It is not a divine right. It is not an accident of birth. Success is a choice." The same can be said for excellence—it is a choice!

THE POWER IS IN THE PEOPLE

Great organizations learn that although technological upgrades are important, the major difference between good organizations and great organizations is always the people who work in those organizations.

It is critical for you to understand the impact that happy people have on great service. Great resorts and hotels make it a part of their service to continually check on the happiness of their employees. Why? Because happy employees tend to give better service. And studies such as those cited in the June 22, 2006, edition of *USA Today* show that if people are happy at home they tend to be happier at work and give better service.

Richard Hadden and Bill Catlette state this concept wonderfully in their popular book *Contented Cows Give Better Milk* (Contented Cow Partners, 2000). They say that those who are happy at home and content in their jobs are exponentially more productive than those who aren't happy at home. Therefore, those who have a higher level of internal satisfaction both at home and at work tend to give better service to customers and enjoy better employee relations. Richard and Bill are absolutely correct: happy people tend to create better results and greater profits for the company.

THE POWER OF LEADERSHIP— AT EVERY LEVEL

In order to have five-star success, you must have effective leaders at every level of the organization. And in order to become a more effective leader, you must become a "Leader of One"! Before you can lead many, you must be able to lead yourself! To become a leader you must stand up on the inside and make the commitment to get better, and then continue to make that commitment on a daily basis.

Martin Luther King Jr. said, "If you don't have something you are willing to stand up for, you will fall for anything!" We all must make the commitment to become more effective leaders; whether entry-level employees or managers or mid-managers. Everyone should be developing into a leader who is proactive and forward-thinking. And I firmly believe that there is a leader in everyone. There is a leader in you!

THE POWER OF "BETTER"

Over the years I have learned a valuable lesson: if any of us wants to have greater success at work and at home, we must make the commitment to get better, to do better, and to be better. In order to experience five-star success, we must be willing to get better in both our professional and our personal pursuits. If we want better children, we must become better parents. If we want better relationships, we must become better partners. If we want better employees, we must become better managers. If we want better results in life, we must become better at what we do, and we must continue to improve on a daily basis.

You've got to make a commitment to get better! I have come to the clear realization that when I started working on myself and working on getting better, my life started getting better.

I was fortunate to hear an interview with Coach John Wooden, the legendary basketball coach of the UCLA Bruins, who won more collegiate championships than any other coach. Coach Wooden was in his mid-nineties when the interview was recorded. In quick succession, he was asked, "Coach, what are you doing every day in your retirement?" and, "Please tell us, what was the secret to your winning so many championships during your time as the coach of the UCLA Bruins?" He responded by saying that he would answer both questions with one answer. "The secret to my success is the secret to my life and is what I have been doing for the last sixty-five years and I continue to do now, each and every day: I work on me! I work on getting better!"

Coach Wooden said that as a young man, he made a commitment to become a lifelong learner and lifelong student of self-development. He discovered that those who have the greatest results over the long term are those who make a commitment to constantly improve themselves. And that those who constantly work on developing themselves will also improve their performance and accomplish more in life. Typically, those who have the greatest achievements are those who make a commitment to continually get better, each and every day.

It was because of Coach Wooden's commitment to self-development that he never became satisfied with success and always tried to improve himself and his performance as a coach. He instilled this philosophy in his players and taught them that no matter who they played against, their biggest opponent was always themselves. He told them our human tendency is to become satisfied with success, and therefore, in time, we create a pathway to mediocrity. Once his players caught on to his way of thinking, they consistently played at another level and consistently continued to improve their performance. That is why Coach Wooden won more college championships than any other coach in history.

For Coach Wooden it was all about constant and never-ending improvement. In the very same way, five-star organizations never become satisfied with success. They are always working on improving themselves and their performance. Pat Riley, who is one of the most successful coaches in pro basketball, said it like this: "Excellence is the gradual result of always striving to do better! Doing a little more every day than you think you can!" Experience has taught me that Pat Riley and Coach Wooden are right: the more I work on myself, the more I win. Plus, the more I learn, the more I earn!

CREATING FIVE-STAR SUCCESS

What does it feel like to be a part of a five-star organization? What does it feel like to live a five-star life? What does it look like in your mind? Are you willing to catch the vision and do the work that is necessary to make the vision a reality? To do what it takes to get "better"?

A great example of this is the Four Seasons Hotel in Washington, D.C., where the general manager, Christopher Hunsberger, developed a new culture of excellence with a concept he simply called "The Better Program!" I read about Hunsberger after the Four Seasons was named one of "America's Best Hotels" in *USA Today* and designated a five-star hotel by the Mobil Five-Star hotel committee. I interviewed Hunsberger and he shared some powerful insights with me about how his hotel climbed from being a very good hotel to one of America's best.

When Mr. Hunsberger became the general manager of the Four Seasons, it was well regarded in the hospitality industry as a very nice four-star hotel, yet he dreamed of creating a world-class five-star hotel. The previous management had tried and tried but had been unable to achieve the five-star rating. Mr. Hunsberger came into the position with his eyes wide open, knowing it would be difficult and challenging, yet he believed it was possible. He set out on a course to make that dream a reality.

He started by selling his staff on his vision of creating a five-star hotel. It was going to take a committed team effort to achieve the goal, and he knew he had to sell everyone in the organization, from the top to the bottom, on this goal. The next step was a major transformation of the physical structure. The Four Seasons underwent a $25 million renovation, resulting in a beautiful facility. Once the renovation was complete, he gathered his staff and asked, "Isn't this a gorgeous renovation? Now what can we do to transform our service to parallel the new look of the hotel? What can we do to create a service culture beyond compare?"

Mr. Hunsberger knew that others could easily replicate the physical improvements simply by spending money. Many hotels have fancy marble in their lobbies and luxurious rooms, but the difference between the good hotels and the great hotels is always the service. Great hotels consistently "wow" the customers with their service. In order to do so, it is necessary to make a commitment to excellence.

Mr. Hunsberger told me that he went to each department and asked the associates, "What can you do on a daily basis to improve service so we can create a hotel beyond compare?" He encouraged them to get excited about developing new ideas, and he reminded them that one of their goals was to so amaze the customers with their service that those satisfied customers would tell everyone they knew about their experience at the Four Seasons Hotel. Hunsberger's better concept focused on "being better and doing better" each and every day. His goal was to create an intuitive service culture that instilled in the associates an ability to anticipate the needs of the customers instead of waiting to be asked.

Hunsberger and his team continued to work on their goal to achieve the elusive five-star award. Year after year they tried and continued to improve but did not receive the highest rating. Even when they didn't make it, they made a commitment that they would keep working on achieving and improving. They created a slogan that they chanted every day—"Five-star or bust . . . Five-star or bust." And they kept getting better.

After five years of working toward their dream, they finally achieved the goal and were awarded the coveted five-star rating. They were written up in national newspapers and industry magazines as "One of the best of the best in the world!" They were proclaimed as "America's Newest Five-Star Success Story." Yet they realized their achievement was not in hitting the goal as much as it was in the culture they had developed in the process. They had created an Attitude of Excellence and a culture of "Better"! And that culture of "Better" was so ingrained in the minds of the staff, that even after they were awarded the five-star status, they continue to find new ways to get better and amaze their customers each and every day.

My friend Zemira Jones, one of America's top management experts, often says: "The harder we are on ourselves, the easier life tends to be on us. Yet the easier we are on ourselves, the harder life is on us!" Or as Lucille Ball, the great comedian and television star, put it, "I have found that the harder I work . . . the more luck I have!"

To become a leader of one you must be willing to stand up and be counted. There is power in realizing your leadership potential. The following excerpt from *A Setback Is a Setup for a Comeback* applies here:

> He who knows not and knows not that he knows not,
> but thinks he knows . . . is a fool! Leave him alone!
>
> He who knows not and knows that he knows not
> is a child . . . teach him!
>
> Now, he who knows yet knows not that he knows,
> is asleep . . . wake him.
>
> Oh, but he who knows, and knows that he knows,
> and uses what he knows, is a leader . . . follow him!

Leadership development is a critical step in the five-star success formula. Are you serious about success, and are you willing to work on yourself to become better? Are you willing to take some classes? Are you willing to attend some educational seminars? Are you willing to take an inventory of your strengths and weaknesses and go to work on improving your skill sets? Are you willing to make a commitment to lifelong learning? Unfortunately, statistics show that most people are more interested in working on planning their vacation than they are on improving self-improvement. They want greater results in life but are not willing to work on themselves. Statistics show that the average person will not read any more informational or self-help books after they finish school. Most people will look at television for hours and never read a book or listen to an educational audio program.

What are you reading? What are you listening to? What skill sets are you developing? I love the concept about lifelong learning that states: "If you ever go to a $10 million home, it will always have a library. The question is, does the person who buys that $10 million home buy it because it has a library, or does her personal library allow her to buy it?"

Again, what are you reading? What are you listening to? What skill sets are you developing? How are you trying to get better? What are you doing to become a better leader? Benjamin Franklin said: "That which we invest in ourselves always pays the best dividends. The pennies we pour into our minds will pour dollars into our pockets."

I am so glad you are reading this book, because it qualifies you as one of the rare ones. Just by picking up this book, you have made a step that the average person will never make. My friend Charlie "Tremendous" Jones was one of the legends in the self-development arena, and he was often heard to say, "In five years you will be the same person you are today except for the people you meet and the books you read!" Therefore, you must take responsibility for your success and make a commitment to work on yourself and become better! If you do this, you will get closer to living your five-star life and developing a five-star organization.

Often people miss out on living five-star lives because they live under the misconception that only a few people are leaders. They believe if you weren't born a leader, you will never be a leader. While it is true that some leaders are born, most leaders are not born but are developed over time. I consider leaders to be like diamonds—they are created through a process. A diamond is initially an ordinary everyday piece of coal that is then separated from the group and goes through a metamorphosis that involves some change, some challenge, some adversity, and some pressure. When it has gone through all of this and comes out of the pressure cooker, it is no longer a piece of coal but a diamond!

Russell Conwell wrote a classic book called *Acres of Diamonds* (Jove Publishing, 1986) that speaks to this in a powerful way. An African farmer keeps hearing about the wealth being generated in the diamond trade. He decides to sell his farm and go out and get rich in the diamond trade. He puts an ad in the newspaper saying he'll accept the best offer. A young man comes out to see the farm, and the farmer sells it to him for pennies on the dollar just so he can get on with his diamond-hunting activities. The farmer searches and searches for diamonds for more than ten years, but he never finds a single diamond. After years of fruitlessly searching he gives up. Destitute and in complete despair, he throws himself off the highest cliff and ends his life.

Meanwhile, back at the farm, the new young owner walks across a waterbed and sees a muddy rock glistening in the sunlight. He picks it up, wipes off the mud, and places it on his mantel. A few weeks later a friend comes to visit from the big city and sees the rock on the mantel. The friend asks if his host knows what it is. The young man replies, "Well, I think it's just a pretty rock!" His friend says, "No! It's a diamond, a big diamond!" The moral of the story is that you do not have to go looking for diamonds because the diamonds are *within you.*

The same is true for leaders. Just as diamonds are not born diamonds, neither are leaders. When a baby is born and the doctor slaps the baby on the bottom, the doctor does not say, "Put this one in the leadership group!" No! The doctor will say: "This is a beautiful baby with incredible potential, and if this baby develops that potential, it can go on and do great things in the future!" The possibilities for that baby are limitless if the baby makes the decision to develop itself. That baby may one day become a world famous doctor, an award-winning educator, or a successful businessperson, or that baby may one day become the president of the United States. The doctor knows that you cannot tell at birth whether the baby will be a great success or not. The potential and possibilities for greatness are inherent in the baby, but at the end of the day the baby's success or failure depends mainly on the choices and decisions that the baby makes.

Of course, circumstances, heredity, and environment play a part in personal development. Yet the biggest part always resides in the person himself.

History has recorded many examples of people who were born into challenging situations, with the odds stacked against them. Yet they overcame the circumstances and achieved great success. In effect, they beat the odds and became diamonds. They became leaders. The potential was within them, but they had to work to develop that which was within them and maximize the potential.

Five-star organizations understand this concept. That is why they invest in their people. Leaders at every level of the organization who think and work like a team inspire greater performance, productivity, and profits. Leaders focus on developing their people by improving their attitude, aptitude, and their appetite. We have learned that one of the keys to leadership development is to grasp the concept that it does not matter where you come from; it only matters where you are going!

3

SECRET 2—PROACTIVE CHANGE MANAGEMENT

Recognize that change is an ally, not the enemy, and develop skills for managing change. If you embrace the components of change, challenge, and choices, you can learn to succeed as you "grow" not just "go," through the changes.

A critical part of the five-star success formula is to accept the importance of change! Leaders understand that you must constantly get better in order to maximize your success, and in order to get better, you must be willing to change. I believe you must learn to embrace what I call the "Three *C*'s for Success: Change, Challenge, and Choices"! Let's look at each of them in greater detail.

CHANGE

Leaders see change not as an enemy, but as an ally. They know that change is going to happen whether we like it or not. Change is inevitable, but our response to change is always optional. We can accept it or reject it; it's our choice!

Imagine change as a supersonic freight train speeding down the track toward us. This train is constantly moving in our direction, in one form or another. And due to technology, change is coming more rapidly each and every day. The computer I bought about a year ago was the fastest and most efficient one available. A year later, when I went to buy software upgrades, I was informed that my computer, "Is just about obsolete!" and was encouraged to simply buy a newer, faster model!

Change will happen whether we want to accept it or not. We cannot stop it from coming, but we can choose how we respond to it. There are several ways we can respond to change. Option one is to stand in front of the train, cross our arms, and say: "I don't want to change. I've made up my mind that I'm not moving! I have always done business this way and it works fine for me!" This is not a good option because the train will run you over!

Option two is to step back and ignore the train, or sit and watch it pass you by, while saying: "Isn't that a pretty train! I've never done business this way before, and I'm not sure about that Internet. I let my kids play on it, though, and I do check my emails maybe once a week." Again, not a good choice because the train will pass you by!

I recommend option three. When the change train comes your way, get on board and ride it! And if you are really wise, you will not only ride it but also find a way to drive it. Jack Welch, the former CEO of General Electric who was often called the "CEO of the Century," was known to say, "Only those who drive change maximize their potential and possibilities!"

Imagine this scenario: a young man who has recently dropped out of college sees the change train coming his way, so he jumps on board. He rides the change train for a short time and then makes his way up to the front. He sees an older gentleman driving the train and asks if he could drive it for a few minutes. Initially, the older gentleman says, "No," but the young man is persistent and keeps asking and asking until the older gentleman gives in. The older gentleman allows the young man to drive, with the stipulation that it can be only for a few minutes.

The young man takes the wheel of the change train and starts driving it. After a few minutes the older gentleman taps the young man on the shoulder and says the time for the test-drive is over. But the young man refuses to turn the train back over to the older gentleman! The young man says he wants to keep driving the change train, and he fights to keep driving. We know him today as a man who continues to drive the change train. He is Bill Gates, the wealthiest man in the world. He proves that Jack Welch was right—only those who drive change maximize their potential and possibilities!

It's been said, "It is best to ride a horse in the direction it is going." I say that you should get on board and ride the change train in the direction it is going, because the change train is coming your way. Remember, you always have the power of choice in terms of your response to change. You can resist it, you can ignore it, or you can get on board and ride it. Change is inevitable, but your response to change is optional. If you are going to have five-star success then you must be willing to change and to see change as an ally, not an enemy. And there are times when change will be thrust upon you. That is when challenge comes into play, which we'll get to later in this chapter.

Change is a part of life and a major part of any successful journey. I am often asked about the title of my first book, *It Only Takes a Minute to Change Your Life.* People wonder if that statement is true: can you really change your life in only a minute? My answer is, "Absolutely!" The minute you make a decision and move in a new direction, that is the minute you change your life. While you might not reach your destination in a minute, you can certainly change your direction. And when you make the decision to change and take action, you change your life!

It Only Takes a Minute to Change Your Life is a book filled with one-minute messages to help people digest change in bite-size pieces! As we move along the path to success, we are going to experience change. Someone put it perfectly when they said, "All progress is the result of change, yet all change is not progress!" Change happens to us all; it is ongoing and never ending. Change impacts and affects each and every one of us, even when we are unaware of it. Management and sales consultant Tom Hopkins says, "If you don't like change, you are going to hate being irrelevant!"

In today's workforce, no one can guarantee that you will be doing the same job the same way tomorrow as you are doing it today. In the late 1990s, I was speaking in Fayetteville, North Carolina, the home of the Fort Bragg military base. The driver of the car service that picked me up had been a military man. I asked him how long he had been driving and he responded, "Just a short while." He explained that he had made a career in the army . . . until they let him go!

"Are you telling me that you were downsized from the army?" I asked.

"Yes," he said and proceeded to give me the details. Initially, he had been very angry—until he had a conversation with one of his friends, who asked about the circumstance that led to his dismissal. He told the friend he had been in the service over twenty-six years and he had done the same job, the same way, for all twenty-six years. He could not figure out why the army would get rid of him after all that time.

The friend asked, "So are you saying you have been doing the same job, the same way, for the last twenty-six years? If that is the case, you needed to be fired. You didn't change, and the world and environment around you did!"

His friend helped him understand that unless you are growing and changing, you are at a disadvantage and are losing your value. To go through twenty-six years doing the same job in the same way is like a person who rides around in a Gremlin car (built from 1970–1978), wearing a polyester leisure suit, and uses a typewriter rather than a computer. As one friend said to me, "If you are not growing then you are just taking up space!"

To thrive and survive in this changing marketplace, you must expand or risk becoming expendable. Some say you must either grow or go! Bill Freeman, the former president of Verizon Communications, told me that he was always encouraging his people to grow. He also said, "If my people are not in demand and have no value outside the organization, they have no value on the inside of the organization!"

Is It Change . . . Or Is It You?

It is uncomfortable to change, because we are creatures of habit. We tend to do what we always do because that is human nature. My mother used to say something to me that helped me better understand the issue of change. She would say, "Willie, if you keep doing what you have been doing, you are going to keep getting what you have been getting!" (After I got enough spankings, I finally figured it out. I needed to change!)

Statistics show that most people who go to a restaurant a second time will get the exact same meal they got the first time. Most people who go to a church, synagogue, mosque, or worship center tend to sit in the same area they sat in the previous time they were there. And don't you dare sit in their seats or you might see them lose their religion! If you go to a gym, you probably have a certain locker that you like to use. And if someone is using it, you may get a little out of sorts. When you put on your pants, you tend to always put the same leg in them first.

We are all creatures of habit, and we tend to do what we've always done because that is the way we have always done it. Yet if you want different results, you must be willing to change. A popular definition of *insanity* is "doing the same thing, the same way, and expecting different results." In order to win in life we must change; if we don't change, we lose, because we don't grow! My friend Dan Burrus, the author of *Technotrends* (Collins, 1994), says, "All living things that will grow, will change. Yet all things that change do not always grow. Whether we have positive change or not is up to us!"

Years ago, noted sports announcer Howard Cosell interviewed heavyweight boxing champion Muhammad Ali, who was preparing to go back into the ring after being away from boxing for a number of years. Cosell mentioned that Ali was about to fight a very imposing adversary, George Foreman, who was unbeaten. Cosell asked Ali: "Muhammad, this is going to be a tough fight. Are you the same fighter you were twenty years ago when you first started fighting?"

Ali looked right at Cosell and said: "I certainly hope not! Anyone who is the same person twenty years later than they were twenty years earlier is a pitiful person!" Ali was not the same fighter. He was older and had changed his thinking and had learned from experience. Ali took on Foreman and implemented a unique technique called the "rope-a-dope," where he leaned on the ropes and let Foreman wear himself out. Once Foreman had grown tired, Ali attacked and won the fight! Ali won the world championship boxing title because he used change as an ally, not an enemy.

One interesting side note about that story and the power of change is that George Foreman also changed! He went from being a big, sulking angry fighter who was mean and uncommunicative, to a pleasant, funny, and personable media personality. He has become one of America's most popular endorsement personalities and the pitchman for the famous "George Foreman Grill." Plus, he went back in the ring and became the oldest man ever to win a heavyweight championship. He reinvented himself and maximized his potential by learning to see change as an ally, not an enemy!

CHALLENGE

Typically, wherever there is change there will also be challenge. Change and challenge often go hand and hand. Even though facing a challenge is uncomfortable, it can also be the catalyst for major growth and development and can ultimately be a key to our success. In his book *Who Moved My Cheese?* (Putnam Adult, 1998), Dr. Spencer Johnson wrote a parable that highlights how people are sometimes so unwilling to change that they end up starving, while those who are willing to embrace change are those who succeed and prosper.

My own story illustrates how challenge can help you find your own success. For many years I was a nightclub singer. I sang jingles during the day and performed in nightclubs in the evenings, where I made the majority of my income. I created a nightclub act that became one of the hottest acts in the Metro DC area. I was awarded the Washington Area Music

Association WAMMIE (the Washington version of a Grammy Award) three years in a row for best jazz singer and best entertainer. Most weekends, we had sold-out performances, and people had to make reservations weeks in advance. I was making money and having lots of fun.

One night after arriving at the nightclub, the club manager told me he wanted to talk to me after the show. I was excited because we had been selling out for months, and the club had made a lot of money. I was looking forward to a raise. I told the guys in the band: "Hey, they finally want to talk! We're finally going to get our raise!"

I walked into the manager's office later that evening and he said, "Willie, you were great tonight! The people loved you! You know we have made a lot of money since you've been performing here."

I was getting more and more excited by the minute. With each word he spoke I saw dollar signs! I was ready to get to the bottom line as quickly as I could. I said, "That's great! So when do we get our raise?"

He said, "Raise? No, that's not why I wanted to talk to you. See, the owners want a better return on their investment. The club is full now, and the only way to get a bigger return on the investment is to cut costs. And since the band is the biggest cost, we are going to make a change." They had come up with something else that was filling up nightclubs for a lot less money. They had bought a karaoke machine!

I asked, "But what about my bills?" That night, I learned no one cares about your bills except you and the people you owe!

I had been replaced by a karaoke machine and I was devastated! I had done everything that I could do to help the owners grow their business. There were radio interviews to promote the club, postcard mailers to invite people, and I even made promotional appearances! I did all of this for the owners, and I never asked for any money because I was trying to help them grow their business. Yet I still got fired, because it was cheaper to have a machine than to have a live band.

I was depressed and upset because all I knew was singing, and once I lost my job I didn't know what I was going to do. It was during this low point that a friend gave me a motivational CD of Earl Nightingale's: *The Strangest Secret*. In it, the author quoted the ancient military strategist Hannibal, the great African (Carthaginian) general who conquered the Romans by doing what the enemy thought was impossible—attacking from behind by way of going over the Alps on the backs of elephants. Hannibal said, "If you cannot find a way, then you must make a way!"

After getting fired I knew I needed to change. So I started a course of self-development, and that experience was the beginning of a new life for me. I began to devour motivational material. I realized I needed to change what I put inside of me in order to change what came out of me—my new thinking, my new action. I wasn't sure what I was going to do, but I knew I had to start moving in a positive direction to get something done. I had a problem, but more important, I had a decision to make. I had to decide whether I was going to keep doing things the way I had been doing them or whether I was going to change. I decided to change! Once I decided to change, my life really did change—for the positive! It was challenging to change, but it was part of the process . . . and it was worth it!

CHOICES!

Once you decide to change, you will face challenges, which are part of the growth process. But understand that it is through the challenges that you grow. We have all heard of "growing pains." All growth is challenging. Babies struggle to learn to walk, yet it is from the falling and getting back up that the baby learns to walk and eventually to run! Will you choose to face those challenges and grow?

Once I decided to choose a new direction I did some things I would have never done in the past. I took a part-time job at Montgomery County Community College where I worked as a counselor for high-risk students. At the end of the semester we had an awards luncheon for the students who had stayed in school and improved their grade-point averages. The director of the program asked me to speak at the luncheon about how we had accomplished the goal. I had no real idea what I was going to say, but as I prepared my presentation, I decided to add an inspirational song at the end, like I was used to doing in my nightclub act.

On the day of the awards luncheon, I delivered my speech and sang my song. The audience gave me a standing ovation. I assumed it was for the song, but after the speech, a number of people came up and asked if they could get a copy of my notes. I was shocked! And because of that speech I received more invitations to speak.

Not long afterward, a member of the District of Columbia Public School System contacted me and asked me to head up a new drug prevention program called "Positive Images." This program was designed to mix music and entertainment as a drug prevention vehicle. I took the job and started working with a group of students who were talented in music and drama to develop skits and musical performances that would project a positive image and positive reasons to stay away from drugs and violence. As a part of the job, I was invited to speak to students and staff at schools about making wise choices. Once again, I added elements from my entertainment years, and my presentations became very popular. I received more and more invitations to speak.

It was during that time that I discovered something within me that I never knew existed: the ability to use words to communicate as opposed to just music. I discovered an ability to speak in public, and because I was used to being in front of people, I had very little fear and I started speaking to more schools. From the school programs, I received invitations to speak for the teachers' association meetings. From the teachers' meetings, many would ask if I could come speak for their church groups. When I spoke at church events, the members would ask if I could bring my message of hope and inspiration to their workplaces. There were invitations to speak from such organizations as Verizon, Martin Marietta, and Marriott, as well as government agencies like the Department of

Transportation, the Social Security Administration, and the Census Bureau. Within a year, I had left my school job and started speaking full time.

Not too long after I started in my new profession, Les Brown, the "dean of motivational speaking," heard me speak and sing. He invited me to be the opening act for his new Music and Motivation Dream Team Tour. This tour featured Les Brown, Billy Preston, and Gladys Knight. They were looking for an opening act that combined those two elements— music and motivation—and I was it!

As a result of being on tour with Les and Gladys, I was introduced to a number of radio executives. I mentioned I had been a jingle singer and had recorded one-minute commercials, so I asked if they would be interested in adopting a short-form radio show called "The Willie Jolley Minute." One executive thought it was a good idea, so we recorded the one-minute shows and started airing them. "The Willie Jolley Motivational Minute" was a hit. After about a year, it was syndicated across the United States.

One day, out of the blue, a book publisher called. He had been riding into work and heard one of the one-minute motivational messages and liked it. He wondered if I would be interested in putting some of those ideas into a book. I said I would have to think about it. Then he started talking about money and I quickly told him, "I just thought about it!" I started writing the book that day!

That first book was titled *It Only Takes a Minute to Change Your Life,* and it quickly became a bestseller. It has gone on to be translated into numerous languages and become a bestseller in Australia, China, Japan, Africa, and India. My second book, *A Setback Is a Setup for a Comeback,* was released a few years later. It too has gone on to become a bestseller and has been translated into numerous languages. A PBS special for teens, "Dare 2 Dream, Dare 2 Win," was recorded not long thereafter. This was a live taping in a high school produced after the Columbine massacre. It has gone on to become one of the top-selling drug and violence prevention video programs for teens in America.

In 1999, not quite a decade after starting my career in public speaking, I got a call from Toastmasters International informing me that I had just been named "One of the Outstanding Five Speakers in the World" for that year! And in 2005, I was inducted into the Motivational Speaker Hall of Fame. All of this occurred because I was fired and replaced by a karaoke machine!

What lesson did I learn? I learned that change happens to us all, but a bend in the road does not have to be the end of the road, unless we fail to change! Stop right here and repeat after me: "Change is good—when your attitude is great!"

Say it again: Change is good—when your attitude is great!

Decide to see change from a positive perspective. Remember: Change is not the enemy; it is an ally! Yet the choice is always up to you!

4

SECRET 3—DEDICATED TEAMWORK

*Embrace the incredible power of teamwork. Those who think
like a team and work like a team are those who win like a
team! Keep in mind that great teams care for each other,
cover for each other, and encourage each other. Everyone is
an MVP—a most valuable and valued player—because the
chain is only as strong as the weakest link.*

*The ancient Greek definition of happiness was the full use of your
powers along lines of excellence!*
—John F. Kennedy

*Great things are not done by impulse, but by a series of small things
brought together.*
—Vincent van Gogh

THE POWER OF THE TEAM

Great organizations understand the power of the team and that to maximize a team's impact the individual members must work together as a well-oiled machine. Lance London, an incredible entrepreneur and owner of the Carolina Kitchen restaurant empire based in Prince George's County, Maryland, is quickly becoming the king of "home style" restaurant dining across the country. He built his business by focusing on great food and great service and by emphasizing great teamwork. I have had him on my radio show a number of times, and he has become known for the powerful statement he shares with his employees: "It takes teamwork to make the dream work!"

Five-star organizations believe in the power of the team. The leaders in those successful organizations further understand this important fact: No one is an island, and no one stands alone! To have success in business and in life, you must make a commitment to building that winning team. Over the last few football seasons, we have seen teams with very few superstars win the Super Bowl! Those winning teams may not have been filled with a roster of superstars, but they had plenty of committed players. Those players were not household names, but they won because they made the commitment to think "Team first." Because of that commitment, they often beat the teams with the big-name players.

Vince Lombardi said: "Great teams do three things: they care for each other, cover for each other, and encourage each other. And that is what they must do in order to win!" If you are going to have a five-star organization, it is critical that you make the commitment to develop a team that thinks about the team first and individual accomplishment second.

PERSONAL BENEFITS OF TEAMWORK

We have all heard the axioms that T.E.A.M. stands for "Together Everyone Achieves More" and that there is no "I" in *team*. But I believe it is more complicated than those clever phrases. Everyone has individual goals and dreams that can connect with the goals and dreams of the organization. The key is for leaders to develop the philosophy that as the team grows and prospers, so can everyone grow and prosper. Likewise, leaders need to inspire the team to see how they can personally benefit from the success of the team members as a whole.

This approach is evident in the story of a young man from North Carolina named Michael Jordan, a first-round draft pick for the Chicago Bulls. When he joined the Bulls, Jordan became a scoring machine and an instant success. He could score anytime he chose to; to prove it, he consistently led the league in scoring. But the team was never able to win a championship because it was a one-man team! No matter how many points Jordan scored for the Bulls, the other team would score more because it was basically one man against a team of five players. Even though Michael Jordan was an all-star defensive player, he could not guard five people. The opponents would come down the court, pass the ball around, and play team ball to outscore the Bulls. And though there were four other players on Jordan's team, they never played like a team; they played like five guys on a basketball court, each doing his own thing. As a result, the Bulls did not win many games.

After a number of seasons of similar results, the Bulls brought in a new head coach who had a new way of thinking: a team-minded approach to the game. This coach's name was Phil Jackson. His very first task was to convince Michael Jordan, and then the rest of the team, that the team that thinks like a team and works like a team is the team that wins.

Jackson spent his personal time with Jordan and shared with him the merits of thinking and working like a team, including that, if the team won, Jordan would personally benefit. At that point Jordan was one of the highest-paid players in the league, yet Jackson was able to convince him of the merits of thinking and working like a team!

Jackson brought in a number of new people, with different areas of expertise, to help develop this new team. Some were ball handlers, some were defensive experts, and some were three-point shooters. But all of them understood that if they kept the team focus and did their individual jobs effectively, the team could win.

The Chicago Bulls went on to win three championships. Then Jordan retired from basketball to play baseball. When he came back to the Bulls, they won three more championships before Jordan retired again and Coach Jackson left to pursue other positions. By the time Jordan finally retired from the Bulls, his personal income was approximately ten times what it was before the team started winning! As the team won, so did Michael Jordan. If you can think like a team and work like a team, you can also win like a team. And you will personally benefit from the success of the team.

I must note here that although you might not make more money when your particular team wins, I can attest that as your team grows, you too will grow. I have worked with a number of government agencies that experienced a dramatic change in productivity and performance after the staff attended my program. I was always amazed when I would revisit their offices and hear all the incredible stories that members shared with me about the impact this concept had on them at home and in their other activities. There will be times when you won't make more money because your team won, but you will be able to use the techniques and strategies you acquire in the organization to influence your family life and community activities.

Here's another way to see it: "It is not so much the goal that you hit but what you become in the process that makes the long-term difference." As the team prospers and grows, so shall you!

A teachable person with a positive attitude can develop aptitude. If you can accept the "good, better, best, never let it rest until good becomes better and better becomes best" principle, then you can develop skill sets that will help you create a reputation of excellence. An Attitude of Excellence and a decision to develop an aptitude or skill set to a degree of excellence are two crucial parts of any winning team's trifecta.

MAKING A COHESIVE TEAM

One of the persistent challenges that occurs in the process of developing great organizations is to blend different people with different backgrounds and different personalities into a cohesive homogenized unit. A critical component of the success journey that is often marginalized is the issue of learning to win with people who are different from you. Some people call this concept diversity; others call it inclusion. But those who understand the science of success call it "Good Business!"

The bottom line in the success process is that it's not about color, ethnicity, or gender—or any other difference. It is really about business and improving performance and productivity of the organization's people! In one of the many interviews I conducted with successful businesspeople on the subject of diversity, a CEO observed: "The number of people of color and different orientation is growing rapidly. I do not see diversity as being about kumbaya but, rather, it is about smart business practices . . . and I am in business!"

The words *diversity* and *inclusion* are often criticized and marginalized because for so long they have been associated with "forced acceptance" rather than seen as good business practices that can positively impact productivity and bottom line profits. A few years ago, I was asked to be the closing speaker for the Society of Human Resource Managers' Annual Diversity Conference. Although I typically speak about diversity, they had heard about my Attitude of Excellence message and asked me to share it. In preparing for the conference, I interviewed a number of diversity experts from different industries. With each interview, I became more intrigued by the information I was presented with.

One expert told me that diversity work is really "mission work" because so many people who are asked to attend diversity trainings make up their minds before they go to the meetings that they are not going to buy into the diversity concepts! They put their sticks in the ground and refuse to change. In essence, there is hesitancy—or even refusal—to change and to operate differently.

Those who lead the diversity operation must be patient and wise and help people see that this new thinking can have a positive impact on their lives and their incomes! Joe Watson, author of the bestselling book *Without Excuses: Unleash the Power of Diversity to Build Your Business* (St. Martin's Press, 2006), wrote: "Diversity, like gravity, is all around us, and is therefore beyond dispute or debate. The challenge of leveraging that diversity and inclusion remains unfinished and unfulfilled! It is hard work!"

Watson went on to say: "Creating a diverse workforce is not about 'being nice' but is rather about creating great business results. Between the pressure of global competition and emerging markets we must appreciate and look at all of the possibilities for continuing to expand and grow our businesses. Diversity and inclusion are not about 'being nice' but rather about using all the possibilities for innovation, and that simply makes sense . . . dollars and sense!"

In my speeches, I share an anecdote that takes me back to my days as a jazz singer when I would split the audience down the middle and teach them how to sing jazz. I would ask the right side of the audience to repeat after me as I sang a simple scat line—"Do Wop!" Then I would have the left side of the audience sing a different scat line—"Do Da!"

I use that same technique during my speeches. After teaching the audience their "parts," I tell them why it is important that I teach them this jazz song in a message about developing an Attitude of Excellence and building great teams.

As I point to each side of the audience, I get them to sing their parts in a call-and-response manner. Finally, I add an a cappella bass line and get everyone singing in a round-robin manner and snapping their fingers and "Presto!"—we have a beautiful song! I then tell them that jazz is a music idiom that was created in America by African Americans. I explain why I believe it is important that we learn more about the African American culture, but we must not stop there! We, as Americans, need to know more about Asian Americans, and Hispanic/Latino Americans, and Jewish Americans, and Italian Americans, and Arab Americans, and European Americans, and all the other people who are part of America.

Why? We might have come over here on different boats, but we are in the same boat now, so we need to learn to row together! Finally, I ask, "Do you see a band standing at the podium with me?" They all say "No," but we all recognize that we just made music! We experienced that when we—people of different ages, different colors, different genders, different religions, different orientations, different educations—all worked together, we made music! It is the same with a symphony orchestra: different types of instruments alone can make individual sounds, but together they can create harmony!

Working together in a harmonious manner creates success and symphonic wonder. On the other hand, being distracted by differences and working against each other creates dissonance and noise! I recommend we learn to work, sing, play, and prosper together!

BUILDING STRONG CONNECTIONS

The next step along the team-building journey is that great teams understand the chain is only as strong as the weakest link; therefore, each "link" must bond with the other links in a solid and secure manner. This connection requires developing a relationship that is trusting and secure among the different links. Each individual within the organization must make the commitment to develop a strong connection with the others so they can collaborate for greater success. They must make the decision that they want to *win* and are therefore willing to get past their individual issues and agendas! This takes a conscious decision to talk "to" each other instead of talking "at" and "about" each other!

To refer once more to the Chicago Bulls, almost everyone knows of their infamous star defensive player named Dennis Rodman. He had a reputation for not being a team player. He consistently did his own thing, which was sometimes detrimental to the Detroit Pistons and the San Antonio Spurs—the two teams he had played on previously. Yet when Rodman went to Chicago, things changed. He became a committed team player! He would occasionally "stray" during his time off, but when he put on the Bulls uniform, he became a committed part of the Bulls' team!

What was the reason for Rodman's change in behavior? It was the Bulls' philosophy about the importance of the team. In Rodman's prior teams, he was criticized and talked "at" and "about" rather than encouraged and talked "to." Playing for the Bulls, he was constantly reminded that there was a benefit to each person on the team if the team won! If Rodman started to drift back into his former patterns, he was reminded that he was a valued and important part of the team. He was appreciated and they depended on him to win!

And it was not just that he was reminded; it was equally important *how* he was reminded, how the importance of his being a team player was communicated to him. There was no talking behind his back or sending of demeaning memos; rather, coaches and teammates were taking time and sitting down with him, person to person, and letting him know that he was valued and important to the success of the team. Once Dennis Rodman was encouraged, then the constructive criticisms that followed were easier for him to take and he was less defensive and resistant.

Believe it or not, many people do not participate in teams because they do not feel they are an equal part of the team and do not feel appreciated. And far too often people hear about their shortcomings through memos or through secret water cooler conversations rather than through open and direct communication from a caring and concerned team member. Talking behind people's backs will lead to an unraveling of the moral fabric of the organization. It is critical across all levels of an organization to be open and honest and upfront about your concerns and not talk behind the back of a coworker.

Steven Gaffney, author of the bestselling book *Honesty Works: Real-World Solutions to Common Problems at Work and Home* (JMG Publishing, 2005), is a member of my Speakers Mastermind Group. This is a group that meets quarterly to share ideas and insights on personal and business growth and development. Steven is one of the top experts on honest communication in America, and in his books he shares that more than 70 percent of the people surveyed in the organizations that he works with—all of which have major issues to address—say they often withhold information or don't tell the truth! Many of these organizations bring him in to help them turn their companies around because of sagging profits.

Steven says that often the root cause of such productivity and profitability problems is that very lack of open and honest communication. Not just the truth-versus-lies aspect but also withholding information and behind-the-back conversations! Plus, this lack of communication leads to fuzzy and blurred goals and expectations. After he has worked with companies on their honest communications, there is a dramatic improvement in performance and profitability.

In order to successfully collaborate it is necessary to cooperate! Steven writes, "Often it is not what team members say that is the problem, but rather what they don't say!" The key is to get the "un-said" said! For example, when people are not performing well, people beat around the bush, they dance around the issue, and they talk behind one another's backs instead of talking directly to each other. If people are not aware of what the problem is, they cannot fix it! This is toxic to teamwork and the growth of any business.

There are three things that have to happen within an organization to help it develop a culture of honest communication.

1. Everyone must be made aware of the problem because you cannot fix what you don't know.

2. Leaders must model the behavior of honest communication. Far too often, leaders say all the right things, but they do not do all the right things!

3. Employees must develop the skill of how to bring up the difficult issues, and they must be willing to be honest and direct, yet caring and considerate.

Open and honest communication can literally transform an organization and help teams grow, even in the most difficult of times.

Simple appreciation is another key element of a successful team. Simple appreciation is a powerful tool for building a winning organization. I believe that most people go to bed each night hungry—not for food, but for appreciation! Appreciation is the simple expression of showing that you value the actions of another. That appreciation can have a tremendous impact on your long-term success and profits!

Some years ago, I was running late for a flight out of Dulles International Airport, near Washington, D.C. I left the office in a hurry (as I often do) trying to get to the airport in evening rush hour. While I was en route, unbeknownst to me, Shirley, my assistant, called the airport to see if they could hold the plane for me! She didn't know I have a deal with the airlines: if I am not there when they are ready to leave, they can leave without me! After calling the airport she called my cell phone and said, "Willie, I called the airport to check on your flight, and they told me it's delayed an hour! Take your time."

Before she hung up I said, "Wow! That's awesome. I won't have to drive like a crazy man, and I can even stop and get some coffee! By the way, I just want to let you know that I really appreciate you." I hung up and stopped for the coffee and got to the airport with plenty of time to spare.

When I finally returned to my office, there was a bouquet of roses on my desk. I assumed it was from a client, but when I read the note, I found that my assistant, Shirley, had signed it! Completely perplexed, I asked why she'd given me the roses. She quickly replied: "Willie, before I came here to work, I worked at the same place for over ten years. Not once in those ten years did anyone say thank you!"

Wow! What a tremendous lesson I learned that day! I learned that a word of appreciation can change lives and encourage and inspire your team members to keep going even in challenging times. If you give appreciation on an "ongoing basis," you will find that the team will grow stronger and stronger.

Another issue that must be addressed is the fact that every person in every organization is going to have times in their lives when life comes crashing in on them at home, and those are the times when we must care for and cover for each other. All of us have problems and personal issues that go with living. That is why I believe that everyone on every team has two jobs—that's right, two jobs! They have one job with the organization and another job when they get home! They might go home to deal with elderly parents, mates who have physical or emotional problems, or *teenagers*!

I don't know what challenges await you at home, but I do know that everyone has some issues that impact their lives, not just at work but also at home. There will be times when you have a specific issue that is so painful you cannot even discuss it! And that is the day when you need your teammates to support you!

A friend of mine who is a very successful corporate executive called recently. His only sister had just died, and he needed a moment to talk with me. He knew I would understand what he was feeling for I had lost my mother and only brother within a twenty-five-day period in 2003. I shared with him how I was able to get through that challenging time and gave him some strategies for healing his heart.

He expressed that this was the most challenging time of his life and that he was having a tough time concentrating at work. Initially, he did not tell his boss about his loss; nevertheless, his boss came to him and asked if everything was okay at home because he was not working with the same efficiency as usual! My friend then told his boss about the death of his sister. His boss asked him if he needed any time off or if he needed anything else to help him through this difficult time.

My friend chose to continue working. He realized that if he stayed home, he would just think about his sister and grieve all day. He wanted to stay at work, and even though his performance was not up to par, he would do the best he could. The boss and the team rallied around him and covered for him. He shared with me how very much he appreciated his boss and teammates. He felt that they went above and beyond the call of duty.

I do not believe his coworkers went above and beyond the call of duty! They did what great teams do: they cover for one another. All of us are going to have those days when we are distracted by a painful challenge, and those are the days when we need the support of our teams to help us make it through. My friend's colleagues did what all great teams do: care for each other, cover for each other, and encourage each other.

Years ago, I read an article about team building that shared lessons we can learn from geese. Geese fly in a *V* pattern because they have a goal: as a team, they know where they are going. They also fly in a *V* because they know if they work and fly together, they can go farther and faster, with less effort, than if they were flying alone. The harder they work together, the higher they fly together.

Then the article observed that geese fly sometimes with the wind and sometimes against the wind. When flying against the wind, the goose at the tip of the *V* has the most difficult job because it has to hit the wind head-on. Yet the interesting phenomenon is that the geese rotate: every goose gets a turn at the lead position. Not only does this allow every goose an opportunity to rest from the challenges of the headwinds, but more important, it allows every goose a chance to get stronger.

Stronger, how? In the process of flying into the headwinds, the goose strengthens its wings—just as we would lift weights if we wanted to get stronger. "The stronger the breeze, the stronger the trees" one old saying goes. It is through adversity that we grow and get stronger.

Another phenomenon about a flock of geese in flight is that they tend to make a lot of noise as they fly. Often, they make so much noise that you can hear them honking from quite a distance. Recently, I was in Williamsburg, Virginia, and I heard a lot of honking and squawking, and I looked up to see a flock of geese flying toward me in their *V* formation. As they passed by,

I realized that they weren't honking and squawking just to pass the time; they were *talking* to and *encouraging* each other.

"Go ahead, Greta, I've got your back!"

"Keep hitting those headwinds, George. We know you can do it!"

Great teams encourage each other. But remember it is important not to talk *at* each other but to talk *to* each other.

If you are going to have a five-star organization, you must develop the power of the team. Care for your teammates, cover for them, and make a point of encouraging them. It will help you win quicker and more often! Coach Lombardi was spot-on: great teams care for each other, cover for each other, and encourage each other!

5

SECRET 4—
WOW CUSTOMER SERVICE

Wow the customer with amazing customer service and your business will grow! As you grow your people, you will grow their capacity to serve, and great people tend to give great service. Remember that the greatest leaders are always the greatest servants.

Do you want to win more? If the answer is yes, then you must ask the question "How do we win more?" In order to win more we must think differently and do differently. We can start by thinking differently about the word *win*. We traditionally think of winning with regard to personal success or to gaining an advantage over another. But I believe there is another perspective we should consider.

Five-star organizations have expanded their definition of *win*. They make a commitment to W.I.N.—that is, to do *whatever is necessary* to serve the customer—because they understand the amazing power of customer service is the key to gaining the ultimate advantage over their competitors! Your commitment to W.I.N.—to do *whatever is necessary* to serve the customer—will be a major part of creating your own five-star success story!

Five-star organizations believe that excellent service is the key to creating long-term success. They constantly focus on how they can better serve their customers. They ask the questions, "How can we improve our service today?" and "How would we like to be served?" The CEO of a five-star resort told me, "We are working to create a business that is so superior in our customer service that we embarrass our competition!"

I'm not talking about good customer service. I'm talking about astounding customer service. Service that makes customers say, "Wow! That was amazing!" If they say it to themselves, they will probably say it to their friends, too. Superior service that astounds is the secret to the success of five-star organizations!

SERVICE IS AN HONOR

While on a speaking tour in Japan, I had an experience that changed my thinking about the incredible power of customer service. Sometimes it is the small things that can make the biggest impact. I have found that some important life lessons about success can be quite simple.

I was on my second tour of Japan to speak to the U.S. Marine Corps—the troops, the families, the children of those who were deployed in Iraq and Afghanistan, and the workers on the bases. At the end of our time in Okinawa, my wife and I were scheduled to travel to Seoul, Korea. When we arrived at the Nagasaki airport for our flight, a representative of Korean Air met us. She bowed as we entered, took our tickets, and said, "Hello! We have been waiting for you!"

I turned to my wife and said, "Wow, this is great! It must be because I was the speaker, or because we have business class tickets." The lady took us through security and handed us off to another Korean Air representative who also said, "We have been waiting for you" as she helped us check our luggage. After our bags were checked, another Korean Air representative appeared to escort us to what she said was the "VIP Waiting Area."

We now felt extra special as we walked toward the VIP room. In order to get to the "VIP Waiting Area" we had to walk past the entrance and the Korean Air representative we had met when we first arrived. As we walked by, we overheard the lady who had greeted us say to another group, "We've been waiting for you!" We then realized that she said that to everyone. When we got to the VIP room, we found that it was a waiting room for everyone!

The Korean Air staff served cookies, small sandwiches, and soft drinks while we waited in the reception area with the rest of the passengers. We were all impressed with the service. It really was first-class service, but little did I know that the best was yet to come.

After a short wait, we were told by other Korean Air representatives that they were there to escort us to the shuttle. They took us through a second security checkpoint, then quickly through customs, and directed us to the shuttle bus. Once we were all on the bus and it was ready to leave for the plane, the entire staff lined up alongside the bus. Every person we had met that day was there, from the Korean Air representative at the terminal entrance to the person who checked our luggage, from the people who took us to the waiting room to the ladies who escorted us from the VIP area. As the shuttle bus was about to pull off, they bowed and said, "Thank you for letting us serve you!" Wow! The next time I travel to Korea, which airline do you think I will request? I'm requesting the one that gave me a Wow! experience.

The awesome lesson I learned that day is really quite simple: it is an honor to be able to serve! Whatever we do for a living, I believe we should do it with a spirit of service. We should see our jobs as more than work; rather, we should view them as an honor and a time to serve. Since that experience in Japan, every time I give a speech I do not see it as work but as an opportunity to serve. I heard it stated years ago: "Service is the rent we pay for our place on this earth!" I could not agree more. So whenever you do what you do for a living, do not see it as work; see it as an opportunity to serve!

Jesus taught that the greatest leaders are the greatest servants. We must not merely give great customer service; we must give awesome customer service. Service that is so memorable that the customer says, "Wow!" and then tells everyone they talk to about it. Yet we can't even stop there. We must bear in mind that every customer is important, whether he or she pays first-class, business-class, or coach-class prices! We must thank them for their business!

Always provide a Wow experience for all of your customers. Make sure to say thank you and let them know you appreciate the opportunity to serve them. In today's complex and competitive marketplace, it will definitely set you apart from the crowd.

My friend T. Scott Gross, author of the hugely popular *Positively Outrageous Service* (Kaplan Business, 2004), says that in today's marketplace we cannot settle for being good or very good; we must strive for Positively Outrageous Service. Positively Outrageous Service is service that goes beyond expectations. It is service that astounds and amazes customers. So make up your mind to W.I.N., to do *whatever is necessary* to astound your customers with Positively Outrageous Service!

"YES" IS THE ANSWER . . . NOW WHAT IS THE QUESTION?

I was in Columbus, Ohio, to speak for the Human Resources Organization of Central Ohio. My friend Stan Robbins picked me up at the airport and said he wanted to go to dinner at the Fish Market restaurant downtown. During dinner, Mike Frank, who is a former president of the National Speakers Association, joined us, and Stan and Mike shared story after story about the restaurant and their incredible customer service. They mentioned how the owner, Cameron Mitchell, had started a chain of restaurants that was focused on great food and incredible customer service. His motto is, "Yes is the answer . . . now what is the question?"

Mike shared a story of how he and his wife were at the restaurant one night and he had a taste for macaroni and cheese, but it was not on the menu. He asked the server if it was possible to have macaroni and cheese, even though it was not on the menu and it was not something they usually served. The server said, "Yes! We can make that happen." And they did! She told the cooks about the order for macaroni and cheese. Because they did not have the appropriate ingredients, they called a restaurant that specialized in macaroni and cheese and ordered some. The Fish Market sent a driver over to get it and bring it back piping hot. Mike said it was delicious and hit the spot, but more important it taught him a valuable lesson about service! Organizations that want to Wow their customers find a way to say "Yes" to their customers!

THE TEN COMMANDMENTS OF SUPERIOR SERVICE

In organizations that thrive on volunteer service (like churches), many workers have the will to serve, but only a few have learned the skill of amazing customer service. Far too often we see great preachers working hard on the message that inspires the listeners, but they are undermined by poor customer service from church workers who are willing but not properly trained to effectively serve at the highest levels. They need the skill to go with the will!

Here are my ten commandments for superior service for those who are employed as well as for those who volunteer.

Commandment #1—Thou shalt serve with a smile.

Most companies stress "service with a smile." Scripture encourages people to be servant-leaders, and those servants must make a commitment to serve with a smile. Why must we smile? There is an old Jewish proverb that states, "A person who cannot smile should not open a store!" It is critical to smile because a smile expresses a sentiment that words do not always express. A smile conveys: "I'm pleased you're here. I want to help you."

It is possible to smile even when you must share information that is not to the other person's liking. For instance, at some megachurches, I have shared that you must smile when you say to parishioners: "I am sorry, but you cannot park there. You must park in the overflow lot and catch the bus." If you can learn to smile even when you have to say no, you will catch the spirit of five-star organizations. Practice saying no while smiling. It will help you as you move to become an effective servant-leader!

Commandment #2—Thou shalt go the extra mile.

A common ingredient of five-star organizations is to always, constantly and consistently, go the extra mile. Let me give you a personal example to illustrate this point.

I was scheduled to speak at government agencies in San Diego, the fourth city of a five-city tour. I arrived at my hotel feeling terrible. I had chills, and my throat felt scratchy. At the reception desk, the hotel clerk greeted me with a note concerning a dinner with my clients that I was invited to attend later that evening. When she noticed I was feeling poorly, she asked whether I was okay. I told her that I was tired and feeling a little under the weather so I was going to forgo the dinner and go to bed. I said I hoped I would feel better in the morning, in time for my program.

Almost immediately after I entered my room, there was a knock on the door. When I opened it, I saw a waiter carrying a big bowl of chicken soup on a tray. He said with genuine concern: "We hope this makes you feel better. Have a good night's sleep!"

The hotel employees had gone the extra mile. The soup was perfect for my travel-weary body. The next morning, I was feeling as good as new.

To refer once more to *Positively Outrageous Service*, author T. Scott Gross writes, "One of the keys to success in serving others is to make a commitment to always go the extra mile with your customers." Similarly, in the Sermon on the Mount, Jesus taught that we should always make a commitment to go the extra mile. "He who compels you to go one mile, go with him two!" In order to create a five-star organization, we must make a commitment to do more than we think is necessary! There is no traffic jam along the extra mile!

Commandment #3—Thou shalt greet, speak, and be real sweet!

Many banks, like Bank of America, Sun Trust, and Wachovia, are now catching the spirit and assigning staff to be greeters at the door. And of course, the number-one retailer in the world, Wal-Mart, has built its business with lower prices and high customer service. They've always had a greeter at the front of their stores to say hello to their customers. There is power in the first impression.

Great organizations don't just greet customers—they talk to them, too. According to customer service axioms, the word *hello* is a powerful inducement for business growth. Just that one word!

Last but not least, make a commitment to be sweet to people . . . *really* sweet. Why? People remember those who are nice, but they love those who are really sweet.

I had the privilege of addressing a men's conference at the Crystal Cathedral in Garden Grove, California, several years ago. Not only did they have greeters and people who went out of their way to speak to you, they also made sure those greeters were really sweet. I visited the bookstore to get a specific book, and I left with five! I didn't really need them, but the people were so sweet that I just couldn't leave—and the longer I stayed, the more money I spent!

Commandment #4—Thou shalt say thank you and please . . . a lot!

One of the most popular inspirational books out right now states, "The most important things you learn about success, you learn in kindergarten." It states that the basics of life are usually the keys to long-term success. In kindergarten, we were taught that we must share and learn to get along with others. We learned that it is very, very important to say thank you and please, and to say them a lot.

In order to have a five-star organization, it is necessary to get along with many different types of people and many different personalities. Say thank you and please often. Those words work as a tonic or oil that smoothes every working relationship! If you want to have a five-star operation, it is crucial that you have five-star manners. Make good manners part of your standard operating procedure. Say thank you and please—a lot!

Commandment #5—Thou shalt be willing to apologize . . . quickly!

Apologizing quickly diffuses potentially explosive and ugly situations. Five-star organizations use the power of apologies and are willing to apologize quickly! They don't delay the apology to prove they are right! For them, the customer is *always* right. Too often, an apology is given only after a long, drawn-out confrontational experience, when there is no other option but to apologize! If the customer is offended or there is a problem, don't make excuses and don't be confrontational; be willing to say, "I'm sorry that happened," even if you are not at fault. Be willing to offer "How can we make this right for you?" right away.

Bill Cates is one of America's premier referral experts. In his book *Get More Referrals Now!* (McGraw-Hill Professional, 2004), he says that clients who share problems and complaints with you should be seen as jackpots that can help you grow your business! They are giving you insight into how to improve your business. I spoke to Bill, and he was happy for me to share the following advice from his book with you regarding how to handle complaints:

1. Say "I'm sorry" and say it quickly. It should be the first thing out of your mouth. Why? Because it costs nothing to say I'm sorry. It is not admitting fault, but simply expressing that you feel sorry that they were inconvenienced.

2. Don't take it personally and get defensive. If you do, you're likely to make excuses and challenge their perceptions. This accomplishes nothing and makes the client feel as though you really are not there for them.

3. Don't argue. Nobody has ever won in an argument with a client. If you "win" and prove you are right, in reality you lose. Don't worry who is right or wrong; see how you can help and find a solution to the problem.

4. Thank them for bringing the concern to your attention. Nothing is worse than having a major problem that others know about, but no one tells you about!

5. When you say you are sorry, say it like you mean it, not just trite words, but sincere sentiment.

A woman from California who had bought one of my books at a local bookstore called our office. When she got home and started going through the book, she realized there was a missing page. She looked on the Internet for my contact information and called my office and brought the missing page to my attention. The problem was that this defective version was created and stocked in stores by my publisher! After I'd finished writing the book, it was technically out of my hands, yet when she called, my staff immediately apologized for her inconvenience and *sent her a new book*! Why? Even though it was not my fault that the book had a missing page and it was technically the publisher's responsibility, *my name was on that book*. People don't really care whose fault it is. They care about being treated kindly and being heard. Make a commitment to apologize, even if it is not your fault. Find a way to fix the problem as quickly as you can.

Commandment #6—Thou shalt anticipate.

Anticipate the needs of your customers. Outstanding organizations don't just respond to the needs of their customers, they study their customers to plan ahead for their next moves or needs so that they are prepared to respond! Here's a personal illustration to show you what I mean.

Often, I meet with clients over a meal to discuss their programs. We usually eat at five-star restaurants. One such restaurant is 1789 in the Georgetown area of Washington, D.C. The food is always great there, but it's the service that's truly mind blowing. They don't just respond to our needs, they hover near the table, waiting and anticipating. Rather than coming around and refilling our water glasses when they are empty, the five-star restaurant wait staff never let the glasses get anywhere near empty! A napkin left on your chair should you leave the table for some reason is replaced with a fresh one. The bread-crumbs are swept from the table and used silverware disappears without a sound.

The five-star organizations are the same, looking for ways to engage customers and meet their needs before customers have to ask. Look for more ways and opportunities to anticipate the needs of your customers, and you will see your reputation and your business grow!

Commandment #7—Thou shalt do what is necessary, not what is comfortable!

To succeed in business and in life, it is critical to go beyond our comfort zones. We must be willing to change and willing to stretch if we are going to grow. Whenever you change and stretch, you will be faced with challenges, both externally and internally.

External challenge is that which we will face whenever we try something new and different. The biggest challenge we face when trying to change, however, is internal. As an old African proverb states, "If you can overcome the enemy on the inside, the enemy on the outside can do you no harm!" That internal challenge is to get yourself to believe that it is possible to change, stretch, and grow. Change is required to grow an organization to the next level. And that change will always create some opposition!

You must make the commitment to do what is necessary— not what is comfortable. I learned this lesson years ago, when I started going from school to school speaking to kids. One day I went to an inner-city school. After going through the metal detectors, I was directed to the principal's office, where I had to ring a bell to be admitted!

The principal looked through the blinds, cracked the door a little bit, and said, "Hurry in!" Then he asked, "How long will you be speaking?"

I said, "About an hour."

He sheepishly advised: "If I were you, I would speak for fifteen minutes. These kids can't handle an hour-long speech. The last person who was here to speak lasted only about fifteen minutes before they got rowdy!"

As I listened to a teacher introducing me, I wondered how I could cut my speech down to fifteen minutes, as the principal had suggested. I figured I could cut out the material on drug prevention, the section on alcohol prevention, and the call for academic excellence and integrity, and just give them some flowery motivational quotes and go! But as I got ready to speak, my spirit spoke to me and said: "What are you going to do today, Willie? Are you going to do what's comfortable or what's necessary?"

Some of these kids had never heard a motivational speaker; some had never heard anyone who came out of this same inner-city environment yet had made a commitment to struggle with school and finish. A person who had struggled with his communication skills to learn how to positively influence people. My spirit spoke to me a second time: "So, Willie, what are you going to do today? Are you going to do that which is comfortable or that which is necessary?"

I started speaking to those young people, and when I finished an hour and a half later, they gave me a standing ovation! I learned a valuable lesson: that in order to grow and make a difference, you must do what is necessary, not what is comfortable! We may need to have a conversation with ourselves as to what the right actions to take are. We know the right actions, but we must talk ourselves into acting. We all have fears—of being embarrassed, being rejected, failing, or being made fun of. Nevertheless, five-star organizations make a commitment to do that which is necessary, not that which is comfortable. So must we!

Commandment #8—Thou shalt take responsibility.

To become an effective leader, you must respond with your ability. To respond with your ability means to be empowered to take the necessary action to help customers without having to ask for permission to do the right thing! To take responsibility is to step out in faith as a leader and to be proactive in dealing with the needs of your customers. And remember, everyone has customers! Customers are the people who give us the reason to operate as businesses.

To take responsibility means to go beyond job titles and job descriptions, to think about what needs to be done, and then to go about doing it! Upon visiting a church recently, I witnessed an usher translating the sermon to a woman of Spanish descent. The usher translated the sermon to this woman word for word! Her job description, usher, did not include translation services, but she made the decision to take responsibility and respond with her ability! In doing so, she reached the guest in a way that the guest could understand and appreciate.

In order to create a five-star organization, it is important that everyone make the same commitment to take responsibility and to respond with their ability. They must make the commitment to not just do their job but to do whatever is necessary to get the job done—even if it is not in their job description!

Commandment #9—Thou shalt lighten the lines!

No one—and I do mean no one—likes lines! Think about it: if you are at the grocery store, don't you look for the shortest line? If you are at a bank, doesn't it frustrate you if there are long lines? If you are traveling along a highway and come upon a traffic jam, with a sea of red brake lights before you, don't you moan?

Statistics show that the main reason people change banks is not because of interest rates or financial concerns, but because of the long lines! Five-star organizations are always trying to find ways to lighten the lines—always.

If the lines cannot physically be shortened, then businesses do the next best thing: they talk to the people in the lines. They apologize for the delays and thank the customers for their patience. The employees make eye contact with the customers in line and say things like, "We'll be right with you!"

Popular five-star organizations, like the Gaylord Convention Hotels in Nashville and the National Harbor complex along the scenic Potomac River in Prince George's County, Maryland, know how to handle lines. When lines form as one group is checking out while another group is checking in, for instance, staff walk up and down the lines and smile and speak to the customers. In addition to thanking the customers for their patience, they recognize the customers and acknowledge that they are important. A few smiles and a simple acknowledgment can do a lot to lessen people's anxiety about the lines. If you can shorten the lines, or at least the anxiety that comes from them, you will grow your five-star status!

Commandment #10—Thou shalt practice the C.Λ.N.E.I. principle.

In the late 1940s, the Japanese were recovering from World War II and struggling to survive. They started creating items to be sold overseas and always stamped the items "Made in Japan." During those times, whenever people in the United States saw that stamp, they knew the items were of inferior quality and could be purchased inexpensively. This practice went on through the 1950s and into the early '60s. In the late '60s, however, something changed.

A management guru named Dr. Edward Demming went to Japan and taught the Japanese an innovative concept called the "Kaizen, or C.A.N.E.I., Principle," which stands for Constant and Never Ending Improvement. It means making a commitment to never be satisfied and to keep bettering your best on a daily basis. Within a decade of embracing this principle, the Japanese had gone from worst to first! Japanese electronics and automobiles dominated the marketplace, and they still do to this day!

Five-star organizations embrace this principle. This commitment to constant and never-ending improvement requires each person to ask, "How can I do better tomorrow than I did today?" Those who achieve great things in life understand the power of self-development and make a commitment to constant and never-ending improvement.

If you were able to achieve perfection, where would you go from there? Constant and never-ending improvement allows us to continue to improve as we strive for excellence. Once we achieve excellence we are automatically compelled to try to constantly improve and better our best!

Great organizations never become satisfied. To create a five-star organization, it is critical to make a commitment to the C.A.N.E.I. Principle. Get started today!

These are what I refer to as the Ten Commandments of Superior Service. If you use them, you will find that they will have a profound impact on your reputation, your productivity, and your profits.

As a guest speaker, I was recently touring Wal-Mart headquarters in Arkansas when I realized that this corporate giant didn't just happen to become the number-one retailer in the world by chance. Their philosophy of constant and never-ending improvement led them to their number-one status. I spoke at an awards banquet one Friday evening and was invited to stay around to attend the managers meeting the following morning. It was an amazing experience to see managers and other employees come in voluntarily on a Saturday morning. But what was even more amazing was how the company philosophy was embedded into the consciousness of those employees!

First, they all participated in the company cheer, which was a chant that goes like this:

> Give me a W!
> W!
> Give me an A!
> A!
> Give me an L!
> L!
> Give me a squiggly! [That is the little dash between the words *Wal* and *Mart,* and all the people do a little twist.]
> Give me an M!
> M!
> Give me another A!
> A!
> Give me an R!
> R!
> Give me a T!
> T!
> What does that spell?
> Wal-Mart!

What does that spell?

Wal-Mart!

Who's number one?

[And the answer blew my mind, because in unison they all screamed:]

The CUSTOMER . . . is ALWAYS number one at Wal-Mart!

That experience helped me understand how Sam Walton's philosophy of customer service took him from a small five-and dime-store in a little city in Arkansas to becoming the biggest retailer in the world. He made a commitment to serve the customer and keep the customer as his number-one focus.

Sam Walton also instilled an Attitude of Excellence, encouraging his employees to constantly pursue doing their best. At that same Saturday morning meeting, I was in awe as the Wal-Mart managers and other employees chanted, "Good is the enemy of Best . . . and Best is the enemy of Even Better"!

I agree wholeheartedly! The race for excellence has no finish line, no end point. With an Attitude of Excellence there is never a point where you are ever "good enough"! Therefore, you must always keep working to get even better than best!

DON'T LET THE ROMANCE DIE

One of the keys that Wal-Mart and many other successful companies understand is the importance that great customer service has on long-term success. What follows is the article I wrote for my online column on Valentine's Day, and the response to it was so overwhelming I thought you also would enjoy reading how success in business and in life are all about not letting the romance die.

It is important to keep in mind that we should not just be thinking of romance around Valentine's Day. We should be thinking about romance all year long! To have a healthy and vibrant relationship, the romance should be ongoing. And in order to keep the fires burning, you must be willing to make an "ongoing commitment" to never-ending romance!

I have been married for over 20 years to the one and only Ms. Dee, and learned early on to commit to never letting the romance die. When I first got married, I had a conversation with an older gentleman, who had been married for over 50 years. He and his wife acted like newlyweds. So I asked him what was the secret to the excitement that he and his wife shared. He said, "Love is not just an emotion, it is decision."

He went into great detail on how to keep those love fires burning. I even wrote about it in the Love Section of my first book, *It Only Takes a Minute to Change Your Life!* Suffice it to say, he taught me that a "happy wife creates a happy life"! He helped me realize that it takes a commitment to romance your mate daily! Not just on Valentine's Day or birthdays, but every day!

Take time out every day to tell your mate that you love them. Make time for a "date night" once a week. Dee and I have been having a date night every week for our 20+ years. When our kids were little, and we could not afford any date nights out, we would have date time in front of the television, with our bedroom door open! We'd eat popcorn, watch television, and talk! It was our time alone, and has continued throughout the years.

We must do the same with our clients. We must work hard to keep that business romance from dying. Unfortunately, many people work hard to get the business, but stop courting their clients once they get their business. My office manager recently changed office suppliers. After she made the change, the old supplier sent an email asking, "What did we do to lose your business?" My office manager simply replied, "You didn't do anything . . . and that was the problem! You worked to get our business and then we rarely heard from you."

Statistics show that it costs twice as much to get new clients as it does to keep old ones. And we all know that in love relationships, it's "cheaper to keep them"!

So work at keeping the romance alive . . . at home and in business! Keep courting them and letting them know you appreciate them. The rewards are endless!

6

SECRET 5 — WORLD-CLASS ATTITUDE ENHANCEMENT

Develop a positive attitude and a positive outlook, in-look, and up-look! Learn to see that change is good when your attitude is great! When it's all said and done, it's all about your attitude!

Some people may have greatness thrust upon them. Very few have excellence thrust upon them. They achieve it. They do not achieve it unwittingly, by "doin' what comes naturally"; and they don't stumble into it in the course of amusing themselves. All excellence involves discipline and tenacity of purpose.
—*John W. Gardner*

Great spirits have always faced violent protest from mediocre minds . . . Continue to pursue Excellence!
—*Albert Einstein*

Be a yardstick of quality! Some people aren't used to an environment where excellence is expected!

—*Steve Jobs*

In my music release titled *Money Making Music and Minutes*, I wrote the lyrics for the song "It's All About Your Attitude" to highlight the fact that everything really is all about your attitude! (My friend Paul Minor wrote the music for this song.) The lyrics are as follows:

First Verse

ATTITUDE . . . One small 8-letter word, yet it has such a big impact on your success or on your failure.

Attitude is not just about a disposition, but also about how you see the World. It's how you see life.

Do you see it from a negative perspective? Or do you see it from a positive perspective?

It's your choice! It's about your attitude . . . It's all about your attitude!

See my friend Keith Harrell wrote a book called Attitude Is Everything.

He was telling the truth . . . attitude truly is everything!

It's about how you view things, how you perceive things, and how you go after things!

Can you control the time? No! Can you control the weather? No!

Can you control what other people say or do? No, No, No!

You can only control YOU and your attitude!

Your attitude to life determines your altitude in life! It's all about your attitude!

Chorus

It's about your attitude.

It's about your attitude.

It's about your attitude.

It's all about your attitude.

Second Verse

Now Dennis Brown says, "The only difference between a good day and a bad day is your attitude."

See, stuff is going to happen, life is going to happen, change is going to happen.

Someone once said, "In life you either got a problem, you just left a problem, or you're on your way to a problem, that's life."

But you've got a choice. You've got a choice how you perceive and how you respond to life.

See, stuff happens to everyone. I wrote a book called A Setback Is a Setup for a Comeback . . . *because that's all it is.*

Setbacks happen to you, they happen to me, they happen to everybody.

But a setback is never the end of the road; it's a bend in the road.

And the only ones who crash are those who fail to make the turn.

It's about your attitude! It's all about your attitude.

Chorus

It's about your attitude.

It's about your attitude.

It's about your attitude.

It's all about your attitude.

Third Verse

Attitude determines your ups and your downs.

A winning attitude means you never frown.

Positive thinking keeps your life on track.

And all good things forward, so don't look back.

See, a bad attitude can turn a bad day worse.

Start thinking good thoughts and watch it reverse.

Good thoughts, Good things, Great thoughts, Great things.

Positive attitude now look what it brings.

Better days, better nights, better job, better life.

Just because you said "I will" instead of saying "might."

Excuse me friend . . . I don't mean to sound rude.

But for real it's all about your attitude!

Chorus

It's about your attitude.

It's about your attitude.

It's about your attitude.

It's all about your attitude.

Fourth Verse

Now as you turn your setbacks into comebacks, you have got to make some decisions.

The first decision you got to make is to decide what do you do when you have a setback?

How do you see it, what's your perspective? Do you see it as a setback period, or as a setback comma?

Setback period means end of a sentence, no more to be said.

But a setback comma means pause, transition, more to come.

You see it from another perspective. And see, if you see it another way, you'll start to be it from another way.

See, you must understand that you must make some tough decisions.

Because you can't control what happens to you, you can't control what happens around you, but you've got complete control over what happens in you!

And you can choose to be happy! That's your choice!

So choose to have a positive attitude.

Next you must make a decision to stay away from negative people.

Negative, small-minded, petty-thinking people who tell you what's not possible for your life. You must make a commitment to stay away from them.

Some of them are going to be in your inner circle. People who you love and they love you, too. They're not trying to be mean-spirited, they just happen to suffer from possibility blindness!

No, you've got to make a commitment to stay away from negative people and live your dreams!

See, folks, you must make a commitment to work on you. If you take a grapefruit and squeeze it, what are you going to get? Grapefruit juice.

If you take an orange and squeeze it, what are you going to get? Orange juice!

If you take a negative person and squeeze them, what are you going to get?

That's right—negative!

You must make a commitment to fill yourself with the pure, the positive, and the powerful! Because your input determines your output!

It's all about your attitude! It's all about your attitude!

ATTITUDE IS THE OIL OF ACHIEVEMENT

Five-star organizations focus on the attitude of their people because the attitude culture ultimately determines the success of an organization! Attitude is the lifeblood that keeps an organization moving. My friend Keith Harrell, author of *Attitude Is Everything* (Collins Business, 2005), says that attitude is *the* crucial factor in all successful ventures.

During his programs, he asks the people in the audience, "How many of you have cars?" Most of the hands in the room go up. He follows up that question by asking, "How often do you change the oil in your cars?" The usual answer is every three months or three thousand miles—whichever comes first. He then asks, "What do you think would happen if you decided to go a year or two without an oil change?" Of course, the answer is that the car would slow down, run sluggishly, and eventually break down!

The same is true for organizations! Attitude is the oil of achievement! If you don't do preventive maintenance on the attitude of the organization, in time the organization will slow down, start to run sluggishly, and eventually break down! There are far too many examples of organizations that have offered no training and no attitude enhancement to their employees. As a result, negative, toxic influences creep in, and before long, the organization falls apart. Negative influences wear away at the fabric of an organization, and without attention to the issue of attitude, those negative influences will unravel the fabric of that organization like a loose thread in a fine sweater!

Aptitude comes second, as we analyze attitude enhancement. Why? Because every director of five-star organizations I've ever interviewed said that a teachable person with a great attitude and limited aptitude is better than a person with great aptitude and a know-it-all attitude! One of the surefire killers of an organization is a person with a funky, negative attitude! That negative attitude is like the flu: it is contagious and will decimate the workplace in no time! Attitude enhancement is critical for success.

Lee Iacocca, the savior of the Chrysler Corporation in the 1980s, once said: "The kind of people I look for to fill our top management spots are the eager beavers, the mavericks, those who try to do more than they are expected to do! I look for those who create a reputation for excellence, and a positive attitude!" People who succeed in the long run are those who have a positive attitude and have created a reputation of excellence over the long haul.

When you have a positive attitude, you will see change differently. Change becomes part of the growth process. You start to see that what is a negative situation for some will turn out to be a positive for you.

CHANGE YOUR ATTITUDE AND SELL YOUR WAY TO SUCCESS

A speaker friend called me one day, and during the conversation he said: "You know I love speaking, but right now we are having difficulty with our sales. Selling really sucks!!" As soon as he said it, I knew why his sales were suffering. I told him: "If you ever want to have success in sales, you must never let those words come out of your mouth again. In fact, you can never let those words enter your thoughts! In order to have sales success you have got to learn to love it!"

I told him I learned that valuable lesson years ago when I was getting started in the speaking circuit and was getting on and off planes every day. At first the travel was fun, but after about a year, the traveling lost its glamour. It was around that time that I had a conversation with my friend Keith Harrell, who was also traveling a lot. I said, "Man, I hate this traveling!"

He quickly responded, "Willie, you can never let those words come out of your mouth again . . . because whatever you speak is what eventually becomes your reality!"

Keith then asked me a very pointed question. "Willie, what do you love to do?"

I answered immediately, "I love to speak and inspire people."

He then continued, "Do you agree that in order to do what you love to do, you might have to travel occasionally?"

I said, "Well . . . yes!"

"Then don't you agree that travel really is the price you must pay in order to get to do what you love to do?" Keith asked.

I said, "Well . . . yes, that's true!"

Keith then concluded, "Then you can never ever say again that you hate to travel because travel is really just a price you pay to get to do what you love to do!"

I shared that story with my friend and told him that he had to think differently about selling. I also told him that when I was in college, I took a class on logic. I learned about deductive logic, which states that if Socrates is a man; and all men are mortal; therefore Socrates is mortal. Using those same lines of deductive thinking, I said to him if he loved to speak (which he told me he loved to do), and if selling was what he must do in order to speak more, therefore logic would say he loved selling!

He was quiet for a few seconds and then he said, "You know what, Willie, you are right!" He then proceeded to proclaim: "I love selling! I love selling! I love selling!" Not long afterward his sales started to improve because his thinking improved. As his attitude toward selling improved, so did his sales and his income!

I like the old story of the young salesman who asked for a meeting with the CEO to discuss a raise. The young salesman said, "I need more money, so when will I get a raise?"

The CEO, who had been in sales all his life, responded, "My friend, your raise will take effect the moment you change your thinking and you become more effective!" As his attitude improved, so did his income! Work on your attitude! Decide to win! Become a product of your Attitude of Excellence and learn to love selling! It will change your life!

LET THE CHALLENGES PROPEL YOUR SUCCESS

Life is filled with challenging times, yet you must not allow those challenges to stop you. Instead, you should let them propel you to your next level of success! In chapter two in my book *A Setback Is a Setup for a Comeback*, I wrote, "Some days you're the windshield, and some days you're the bug!" Some days everything goes your way, and some days you are faced with "1-800-Brickwall." But don't despair. Every day you wake up you get to choose. You can choose to be a negative bug or you can choose to be a positive bug. And on those days when life throws brick walls at you, you still have a choice as to what kind of bug you will be and how you will respond to the challenges facing you. It is your choice!

The negative bug wakes up, starts its day, and hits a windshield. It doesn't like the windshield, nor does it deserve the windshield. The negative bug reacts to the situation by crying and whining about the bad things that are happening, telling everyone who will listen how horrible life is. The negative bug makes a habit of complaining. It doesn't know the real deal about complaining: 80 percent of the people you complain to simply don't care, and the other 20 percent are just glad that what you're describing is not happening to them! Eventually, the negative bug creates a downward spiral and smashes, crashes, and burns.

Likewise, the positive bug wakes up, starts its day, and hits a windshield. It doesn't like the windshield, nor does it deserve the windshield, yet it has a different attitude and has a different response. The positive bug realizes that the major key to long-term success is that although it cannot control what happens *to it,* and it cannot control what happens *around it,* it nevertheless has complete control over what happens *inside of it!* Positive bugs choose to be positive; they choose to be happy. They refuse to let anything or anyone take away their joy! That is their choice! As a result of their choice (namely, to maintain a positive perspective), they develop a force called resiliency, the ability to bounce back from adversity and difficult situations.

While the negative bug smashes, crashes, and burns, the positive, resilient bug bounces off the windshield! When the positive bug bounces, it hits a higher trajectory and flies above the windshield. Occasionally, a tractor trailer will come along and hit that bug, but that is just another opportunity for the positive bug to fly higher!

Stuff will happen and change will happen, but ultimately it is your choice as to how you respond to it. So don't take stuff personally, and whatever you do, don't let it stop you! Don't just *Go* through it; learn to *Grow* through it!

In the book *The Road Less Traveled* (Touchstone 25th anniversary edition, 2003), by Dr. M. Scott Peck, the first three words say it all. "Life is difficult." Yes, life is challenging, but life is wonderful and awesome at the same time! I'm even working on a new book that says, "Life does not have to be perfect to be wonderful!"

Success is a choice, and if you really want to succeed and live a life of five-star success, it all comes down to making good choices and not letting your life be governed by default. In other words, it will come down to your choices—and your attitude is your choice! You must make the choice to stay positive in spite of the challenges of life.

DON'T WAIT FOR YOUR SHIP TO COME IN . . . SWIM OUT TO IT

Many people speak about how they are waiting for their ship to come in. They patiently sit and wait for their break to come. I remember my days as a nightclub performer (long before the days of *American Idol*) and how I was always waiting for my "Big Break," waiting to get "discovered." (I didn't realize that most of the people in the nightclub were too drunk to discover their way out the front door, much less my talents, as I stood on the stage singing my heart out!)

I had always heard people say, "Just keep singing; sing real hard, and one day somebody will give you a break!" I kept waiting for my break, but it never came. Then I learned to stop *waiting* for my breaks and start *making* my breaks. I learned that success is a choice that you must make happen, not a chance that you sit and wait for. I love the old Chinese proverb that states, "He who waits for roasted duck to fly into his mouth . . . waits a long, long time!"

I learned that the best way to grow your future is to first grow yourself. I started a program of self-development. I had a choice. I could continue to wait for my ship to come in or I could swim out to it. I decided to swim out to it, and I am so glad I did because some of my friends are still standing at the pier, waiting. Jonathan Winters said, "I kept waiting for success, but it didn't come, so I just went on without it."

Folks, success is not a thing that you wait for—it is a thing you achieve! Don't just wait for your ship to come in; jump in and start swimming to it. Make a commitment to be proactive about your success. Make a commitment to take action today on your dreams and your goals. Make a commitment to read and listen to something positive and uplifting each and every day. For example, I listen to motivational music each and every morning, and it has a profound impact on my spirit and my psyche. I specifically make a point to listen to my song "You've Gotta Keep Kicking" because it gets me pumped up and reminds me that amazing things happen in life when you keep kicking and don't give up. (*Note*: Please feel free to visit my website at www.wjspeaks.com and listen to free samples of the motivational music we have created. It will help you start your day with a new attitude! You'll be glad you did!)

I recommend that you work on your attitude *before* you need it, because sooner or later you will need it. I believe that strong faith and a positive attitude can get you through the tough times and help you maintain your sanity in the midst of insane times. Just because life is crazy does not mean you must get crazy with it!

In my latest book, *Turning Setbacks into Greenbacks*, I share a story about our car catching on fire and how people were amazed when they saw how calmly I responded to it. Yet they did not know that the reason I was able to stay calm in a crazy time was because I had dug my well deep before I was thirsty.

My wife and I were at church one evening at a Bible Study when someone rushed in and said, "Willie, your car is on fire!" We rushed to the parking lot and sure enough, our car was on fire. It was ablaze!

According to the police, my wife's car had started smoking about half an hour before the fire started. When sparks and flames began to come from under the hood as well as the dashboard, the police immediately called the Fire Department. But because the electrical system was burning and thus disabled, firemen could not open the doors or the hood of the car. They had to use an axe to break open the windows and to get the hood open to put out the fire.

As we stood there watching our car being consumed by flames, someone asked how we were doing. I said: "I am blessed and grateful! This is nothing but a minor setback, and a setback is nothing but a setup for a comeback!"

"You really believe that stuff you talk about, don't you?" he asked.

I replied: "You're absolutely right! This is not a big deal! See, this car could have caught fire while my wife was driving to a conference earlier this week, or when she picked me up from the airport, or while we were driving to church tonight! I am blessed and so very grateful! And, I know the world will not end. It is just a car. I can replace a car. I can't replace my wife! This setback is nothing but a setup for a comeback!"

The great poet and mentor to Oprah Winfrey, Maya Angelou, said: "If there is something in your life you don't like, then you should change it. But if you cannot change it, then you must change your attitude!" Choose to have a positive attitude, even in the midst of negative, difficult times. Choose to live your dreams and a life of five-star success!

I was asked what you should do if you hit the tough times before you have worked on your faith and attitude. My response is, "Start where you are!" In other words, the best thing to do when you are in a hole is to stop digging and start climbing. Start where you are and keep working on your attitude and your faith. It will help you rise up and out.

GET HUNGRY

The third part of attitude enhancement is that you must have appetite! Appetite is your desire for your goals. What level of desire do you possess? What are you willing to do? How badly do you want to win? Are you hungry?

Les Brown recorded a PBS special entitled "You've Gotta Be Hungry" that shared his story of fighting for his dream of becoming a radio announcer, even as he was going from failure to failure. It was his hunger and his desire that helped him become a successful radio personality before becoming a world-famous motivational speaker and author. So, my question to you is, "Are you hungry for success?" What are you willing to do to achieve your goal?

This is an important question in the quest for five-star success. Imagine that someone takes you out to Giants Stadium in the Meadowlands of New Jersey. And while you are standing in the middle of the field, the person says to you, "There is a treasure worth millions of dollars buried somewhere in this field, and I am offering you an exclusive opportunity to find it and claim it!" Would you be willing to start digging? I assume most people would say, "Yes, I would be willing!" The challenge is that you don't know where on that big field the money is buried. You very well could be digging for quite a while! The key to finding the money is the willingness to keep digging.

I contend that the same is true in life: you must keep digging for your millions! I believe that there are millions of dollars with your name on them, waiting for you to come up with an idea, product, or service that the world will pay you for, yet you must continue to keep digging. I don't know where the treasure is buried, but I do know where the key to the treasure is—the key is within you! And you must be willing to keep digging for it. Bishop T. D. Jakes says: "Many wondered and talk about the fact that I just appeared one day and had success, but they did not see the years and years of struggle in the back hills of West Virginia. Everything I have achieved is a result of struggle and working hard to reach my goals. I have continued to dig and dig and dig! So when I die, make sure to look up under my fingernails. You will find dirt under my fingernails because I will be digging until the absolute end!"

I encourage you to keep digging and to keep pursuing excellence as you go after your dreams and your goals. You must want it badly and you must have a strong appetite! To live the five-star life and have five-star success in your professional and personal endeavors, you must develop a five-star mind-set and a winner's attitude. You must develop an appetite to win!

Feed Your Will to Win

The difference between a successful person and others is not a lack of strength or knowledge, but rather a lack of the will to win!
—*Vince Lombardi*

When we think of winning we usually think about those who are first in a contest, but that is not the totality of winning. Winning is also about overcoming our own self-limiting beliefs and making a personal commitment to fight through the challenges in order to achieve a goal. Webster defines *winning* this way: "to gain or get possession of by exerting great effort."

Winning is not just about being the best or finishing first. It can also be about moving forward in the face of overwhelming odds. A person who finishes a marathon without legs and finishes dead last is a winner. A single mom who decides to go back to school and get a college degree while still working a full-time job and raising her family is a winner—no matter how long it takes her to do it. The small businessperson who hits a rough patch and goes deep into debt and loses all his savings, yet comes back, starts over, and turns a profit—that person is a winner! Winning is not just about finishing first.

It takes great effort to win in life. The reason most people do not win is because they are not willing to exert enough consistent effort. Many people sincerely go after a goal and work really hard at it for a while, but then they fall off and, eventually, give up. As I have studied successful people over the years, I have been amazed by the similarities in those who consistently win. These successful people are not extraordinary personalities; rather, they are ordinary people who do extra-ordinary things and thus become extraordinary! They are people who start out after a goal and refuse to give up until they achieve that goal. They are the people who make up their minds that they are not going to stop. This is the key to their success: they make up their minds! That's right, the first key to developing the winner's edge is a made-up mind!

MAKE UP YOUR MIND

Most people do not succeed in life because they do not make up their minds. They never make the commitment to win. What hinders most people in the quest for success is commitment. We talk about wanting to succeed and we think about success, but we don't jump in with everything we have within us. William H. Murray wrote in *The Scottish Himalaya Expedition* (1951)

> Until one is committed there is hesitance, the chance to draw back, always ineffectiveness. Concerning all acts of initiative (and creation), there is one

elementary truth the ignorance of which kills count-less ideas and splendid plans: that the moment one commits oneself, the providence moves too. A whole stream of events issues from the decision, raising in one's favor all manner of unforeseen incidents, meet-ings and material assistance which no man could have dreamt would come his way. I learned a deep respect for one of Goethe's couplets: Whatever you can do or dream you can do, begin it! / Boldness has genius, power and magic in it.

It takes that commitment to win, and that begins with a made-up mind. Make up your mind; commit yourself and then get busy! This is how you get the will to win!

CONCLUSION

In part one of this book we have talked about the following ideas:

1. Develop the leader within. Remember that before you can lead many, you must be able to lead yourself.

2. See change as an ally, not as an enemy. If you understand the components of change, challenge, and choices, you will learn to succeed as you grow through the changes, not just go through them.

3. Develop the team: learn to think like a team and work like a team so that you can win like a team. Keep in mind that great teams care for each other, cover for each

other, and encourage each other. If you can do this, you will see that five-star success is not just for a select few but possible for every organization and every person in the organization.

4. Embrace great customer service; live the "Ten Commandments of Superior Service." Service is the rent we pay for living on this earth. The more we serve, the more success we will have and the more our lives will be fulfilled.

5. Finally, develop a positive attitude. Change is going to happen whether we like it or not, so those who accept the principle that "change is good when your attitude is great" succeed more often and enjoy the process more often!

PERSONAL DEVELOPMENT: FIVE SIMPLE STEPS TO FIVE-STAR SUCCESS

7

FIVE SIMPLE STEPS FOR
YOUR SUCCESS

The chapters in part 2 are the second half of a two-part program to create extraordinary organizations by growing the people who work in those organizations. These chapters are designed to help you develop your personal power and your personal potential and possibilities as you grow your Attitude of Excellence. Your personal power positively or negatively impacts the success of the organizations that you are involved with. The messages in these chapters will positively impact the results that you are able to achieve in your personal life that will also impact your professional life.

Let me say at the beginning of this section that these literally are simple steps. You don't need to be a rocket scientist or a nuclear physicist to understand the steps. If you apply these simple steps they will positively impact your life and you will see substantial results in a short time.

The best part about these steps is that they are not a big secret or a mysterious formula; they are simple steps that you probably have some familiarity with. You just need to be shown a different perspective. So let's get it on!

DO YOU WANT MORE IN THE FUTURE?

First I must ask you some preliminary questions.

> Do you want greater success?
>
> Do you want more in the future than you've had in the past?
>
> Do you want to be more in the future than you've been in the past?
>
> Would you like to make more money in the future than you've made in the past?

Most people say they want to do more, to achieve more, and to make more money, yet most don't know how to accomplish it. I understand that. I struggled with that as well. I was bewildered by the questions and decided that I would dedicate myself to finding the answers.

For years I searched for the answers. I sought out some of the greatest teachers and success experts, trying to come up with a solution to this problem. I am excited to say that after years and years of seeking and searching, I have come upon an answer to the puzzle. Not only have I found a solution that works, it is also simple. A solution that is simple yet powerful! I have entitled it "Success Made Simple" because that is exactly what it is: a simple solution for success. In the chapters that follow I outline five simple steps you can take to create five-star success in both your personal and your professional endeavors.

FIVE SIMPLE STEPS FOR FIVE-STAR SUCCESS!

We all have ideas that pop into our heads that could literally transform our lives, yet most people disregard or ignore these ideas. I like to ask people in my programs this question: "How many of you have had at least one good idea in your life?" And most everyone raises a hand! Then I ask, "How many of you have talked yourself out of one good idea?" And again, most people nod and raise their hand. Finally I ask, "How many of you have had an idea that you knew was a good idea, yet you didn't move on it, and a year or two later you saw someone else living your idea?" Now, most of the hands really go up! Typically, we think about the idea, but we do not move on it because we have not sold ourselves on the idea.

Many people are just going through the motions of life, like a robot. They get up, go to work, come home, watch television, and go to bed. John Alston, my friend, fellow speaker, and author, shares something similar in his speeches, when he steps from side to side and backward and forward on a stage to underscore each point: "Most people get up (step forward), go to work (step to the side), come home (step backward), and go to bed (step to the other side)." Of course, if they are working mothers, they have an additional step. They get up, go to work, come home, go to work, and then go to bed! Most people have a routine that ends each day back where they started.

Day in and day out they do the same thing and consistently get the same results week in and week out. Some have described this behavior as a form of sleepwalking or like walking on a treadmill: the person is moving but not really going anywhere. They are in a state of merely existing or surviving when they should be in a state of thriving!

We must wake up to the possibilities for our lives. We must wake up mentally and think differently!

8

STEP 1—WAKE UP . . . AND DREAM!

First, let's explore what it means to wake up. Some years ago, Teddy Pendergrass sang a popular song whose lyrics compared sleeping with backward thinking and waking up with thinking ahead. If you are going to live life to the fullest, you must not allow yourself to settle for mediocrity. Instead, you must wake up to the tremendous possibilities that are available to you. You must wake up to the fact that you can actually live a life that is incredible and awesome—but that it's up to you!

WAKE UP THE WINNER WITHIN

Dorothea Brande wrote a book called *Wake Up and Live!* (Simon and Schuster, 1936) in which she extolled the virtues of looking at life through different lenses. She said, "We need to realize that there are incredible opportunities and possibilities all around, within our grasp, if we would just wake up and live!"

You must make the commitment to live life to the fullest and take advantage of all the wonderful things life has to offer you. Those who make the commitment to succeed realize that they can, and should, live life to the fullest. And that they should do it now!

Frank Sinatra once said, "You should live your life full out, like it is your last day—because one day you will be right!" My godmother in the speaking business, the late great speaker and singer Rosita Perez, liked to put it this way: "Don't take your music with you to the grave. Live full, die empty!"

Unfortunately, most people do not live life to the fullest. They want more *out* of life, but they are not willing to put more *into* life. They live their lives sitting in front of a fireplace saying, "Give me heat," without adding any wood, and without even starting a fire! Far too often we live life like the sports teams that are so afraid to lose they never even try to win. In my newest book, *Stop Playing Small: If You Want to Win Big, You Have Got to Play Big!* I confront my own fears and self-limiting behavior.

I ask myself the following questions:

1. What do you want?

2. What are you doing to get what you want?

3. What are you *not* doing to get what you want?

I encourage you to have an honest conversation with yourself and confront your fears. Tell yourself to stop playing small!

In 1956, Earl Nightingale, a popular radio host and success coach, recorded the landmark self-help program *The Strangest Secret* (which I mentioned in chapter 3 as having been influential at a critical point in my life). He stated that most people are doomed to failure because they are like robots in the process of following the leader. Unfortunately, the leaders they are following don't know where they are going, and it becomes a hopeless game of the blind leading the blind! He quoted the noted psychiatrist Rollo May, that the "opposite of courage is not cowardice, it is conformity."

Nightingale took that idea a step further: "Less than 5 percent of Americans are wealthy . . . in the wealthiest country in the world. Most people today are living a life of conformity, where they conform to the populace. Unfortunately the populace is going in the wrong direction" (*The Strangest Secret* recording, 1956).

This is evident in our country today, still the richest the world has ever seen. Yet many people in America are not able to take advantage of the great opportunities that are available. Statistics show that people from other countries become millionaires five times faster in America than those who are born here. Why? Those emigrants may come from a country where they made five dollars a day and when they come to America they realize they can make five dollars an hour! They get busy. They come and live the American dream before those who are born here even realize there is an American dream! I can attest to the fact that the American dream is alive and well, but you must first be willing to dream!

AFTER YOU WAKE UP, THEN DREAM!

Wake up and dream? You might say this is an oxymoron. How do you dream while you're awake? This might sound strange. In order to have success and live life to the fullest you must wake up—and then dream! I want you to grab your vision and see that this is a great time to be alive. Get a vision for your life and get excited about all the wonderful opportunities and possibilities that are within your grasp. Get excited about the fact that you are still in the land of the living! Therefore, you have an opportunity to change your life for the better. In fact, you have an opportunity to live the absolute best life ever!

Not only is it possible, but those who are able to master this skill are also those who have the greatest success. For years I have shared that dreams are the seeds for success. I have given examples of people who were willing to dream and how those dreams helped them achieve great success.

When Michael Jordan was asked in an interview to describe the secret to his incredible success on the basketball court, he gave an answer that has become legendary in his own time. When he was in high school he got cut from the basketball team for not being good enough. He went home and started dreaming about doing impossible things with a basketball in order to prove that the coach had made a mistake. Once Michael saw these incredible basketball exploits in his mind, he went out on the court and replicated what he had dreamed about. He said that once he saw the basketball move in his mind, he realized that he could do it on the court. He found that he could achieve those things that he dreamed about.

And he went on to be called the greatest basketball player that ever lived.

Duke Ellington was asked what was the key to his success as a musician. He responded, "I dreamed a lot!" Walt Disney was asked how he was able to go from being bankrupt and suffering two nervous breakdowns to creating Disneyland and becoming a multimillionaire. He responded, "I kept on dreaming!"

Muhammad Ali was asked how he revolutionized the boxing industry so that people would flock to see him box. He answered: "I used my imagination and created a personality that people either loved or they hated! Those who loved me came to see me win! Those who hated me came to see me lose. In the meantime, every seat was taken!" Albert Einstein said it so aptly when he declared, "Imagination [what I call the power to dream] is much more important than knowledge." Those who have the greatest success are those who are able to dream the greatest dreams.

You have got to have a dream! The bigger your dream, the bigger your rewards. Most people go through life never realizing the great potential and possibilities that lie within themselves. Ralph Waldo Emerson said, "That which is before you and that which is behind you can never compare with that which is within you." We live in a time of unlimited opportunities and possibilities, yet most of us never wake up and dream. Therefore, we don't recognize the greatness that is within us.

Many people downplay the importance of dreaming because at some time in their lives they have been cautioned by a "caring" friend or loved one to stop dreaming and get real. I say "caring" friend or loved one with tongue in cheek, because many of the people who kill our dreams are not enemies or foes, but our friends and loved ones. They are not being mean-spirited; they just suffer from possibility blindness—like I wrote in the song "It's All About Your Attitude."

Stay away from negative people, even those who say they are your "caring" friends. They can and will kill your dreams!

Not only must you start dreaming, you must also continue to dream and keep dreaming big! Studies show that people with dreams and goals live longer than those who don't have them.

The importance of the concept of waking up and dreaming became evident to me in a vivid way when I was about to release my second book, *A Setback Is a Setup for a Comeback*. I had approved the blue lines, and the printer was about to get the green light to start the print run, when a friend sent me a quotation that was so profound I had to have it in the book. I read the quotation and immediately picked up the phone and called my publisher.

"Please, stop the presses!" I said. "I have something that has to go in the book!"

I am so glad the publisher accepted the additions. I was really inspired by the following words of T. E. Lawrence (better known as Lawrence of Arabia), and so were thousands of others who have commented to me in person or via email.

> All men dream; but not equally. Those who dream by night in the dusty recesses of their minds wake in the day to find that it was vanity; but those that dream by day are the dangerous ones, for they may act out their

dreams with open eyes, to make it possible. (*Seven Pillars of Wisdom*, Doubleday, 1926)

You must have a vision if you are going to live life to the fullest. You must catch the vision! Scripture says, "Where there is no vision the people perish," and I believe that where there is a vision the people will flourish. You must have a vision! Helen Keller was once asked, "Is there anything worse than total blindness?" She answered, "Yes! It is a terrible thing to see and have no vision!" Your vision is a critical component to living the five-star life and enjoying five-star success.

It is hard to live life to the fullest if you haven't conceived what that kind of life would look like. If you do not have a vision in your mind, and you do not know where you are going, how can you ever achieve it? It is like the scene in *Alice in Wonderland* where Alice comes to a fork in the road, looks up in the tree, sees the smiling Cheshire cat, and asks him which road she should take. The Cheshire cat inquires, "Where are you going?"

Alice replies, "I don't know!"

The Cheshire cat says, "In that case, any road will do!"

Most of us are like Alice; we are working hard, but sometimes we have no specific goal. In other words, we are going through life, yet when all is said and done, we don't know where we are going.

In order to live life to the fullest, it is absolutely necessary that you start with your dreams. They are the seeds for success. If you took a corn seed, dug a hole, planted it, and watered it, in time it would become a corn stalk. If you took an acorn, dug a hole, planted it, and watered it, in time it would become an oak tree. The same is true for your dreams.

If you can dream, and then plant that dream in your heart and water it continually, in time your dream will become a reality. But you need to know how to water the dream. You must water it by constantly saying: "I believe I can do it! I believe I can do it!" You must do this on good days and bad days, happy days and sad days, sunny days and rainy days. You must continue to affirm that your dreams can come true. If you do then your dream will grow, blossom, and burst into being.

My good friend Al Walker, the great speaker and humorist, shared with me a lesson about the power of visualization he learned from watching the movie *The Karate Kid*. In the film, a young man named Daniel had moved to a new area with his mother and was trying to fit in, yet he was having difficulty. One day while going home from school on his bicycle, he was attacked by the local bullies, who tore up his bicycle. They were ready to tear him up, too, when out of nowhere a man who knew martial arts came to his rescue and beat up the bullies, allowing Daniel to escape. This man was Mr. Miyagi, and he became Daniel's friend and mentor.

In one scene, Daniel was in Mr. Miyagi's backyard, where Mr. Miyagi was carefully clipping a bonsai tree. Daniel was very impressed with the tree. He asked Mr. Miyagi where he had learned such a fine art. Mr. Miyagi told Daniel that he had learned it when he was about Daniel's age. Mr. Miyagi then told Daniel that he would teach him to do the same.

Daniel proclaimed that he was not talented with art and that he couldn't do it. Mr. Miyagi told Daniel that he could teach him the fine art, but again Daniel declined, stating that he was not talented enough. Mr. Miyagi insisted: "I can teach you! You can do this!"

But Daniel again stated, "No, I can't. I am not talented enough!" Back and forth this conversation went, until Mr. Miyagi told Daniel to stop and take a good long look at the plant. Daniel looked at it intently, and then Mr. Miyagi told Daniel to close his eyes. Daniel closed his eyes and Mr. Miyagi said, "Can you see the plant in your mind?"

Daniel replied, "Yes!"

"Can you see it clearly?"

Daniel again said, "Yes!"

Mr. Miyagi said, "Can you recall the detail and the indentations?"

Daniel again responded, "Yes!"

Finally, Mr. Miyagi asked Daniel to open his eyes. When Daniel opened his eyes he saw that Mr. Miyagi had replaced the finished, clipped bonsai tree with an unfinished, unclipped bonsai tree. He said, "Daniel, now I want you to work on what you just saw in your mind!"

The moral of the story is that you cannot *be* what you cannot *see*. You must have a vision!

9

STEP 2—SHOW UP!

You must show up! That's the next step necessary to live life to the fullest. That's right, you have to show up! Woody Allen said that 80 percent of success is simply showing up—and he was right!

SHOW UP WITH YOUR STUFF

I learned this lesson when I got started in the speaking business. As I mentioned in chapter 3, Les Brown and Gladys Knight invited me to be part of their Music and Motivation Dream Team Tour. I was always nervous before each event. One night while waiting for the show to begin, I was in the green room flipping through the channels on the television. The face of a woman I knew came on the screen. She was on the television selling tapes on "how to have successful relationships." She was calling herself "a relationship expert." My mouth dropped open. I said out loud: "How in the world can she talk about relationships? I know that lady! She's been married five times!"

Les laughed and said, "Willie, the reason she is there is because she showed up!" And Les was right. I knew people who were more qualified than she was, but they didn't show up. People who have had lasting and loving relationships did not show up—she did!

Make the commitment to show up and move in the direction of your dreams and goals. Once you show up, make the commitment to continue to keep showing up. Show up with your stuff! Show up engaged! Show up excited! Show up and take it to the next level—on a daily basis. Show up energized and enthusiastic about your job or whatever tasks you are expected to perform. Show up ready to get busy. Make a commitment to your commitment and keep showing up.

Many people do not succeed in life, not because they do not have the talent or the ability to do great things, but because they simply do not decide to show up. I have found that if you do more than you are expected to do, go farther than you are expected to go, dig deeper than you are expected to dig, and give more than you are expected to give, good stuff happens for you.

Over the years I have learned the truth that if you do more than you're paid to do, one day you will be paid more for what you do. As my buddy Les Brown says, "If you do the things today that others won't do, you will have the things tomorrow that others won't have!" I want to encourage you to show up with your stuff and show up with an attitude to do more than you are paid to do, and one day you will be paid for more than you do!

Many times, the reason people don't succeed in life or business is not a lack of talent, skills, or abilities; they simply don't show up! They don't show up and let the world know that they are there and have something to say.

Author and educator Dennis Kimbro states:

- If you show up . . . you get the business 80 percent of the time.
- If you show up on time . . . you get the business 85 percent of the time.
- If you show up on time with a plan . . . you get the business 90 percent of the time.
- If you show up on time, with a plan, and implement that plan . . . you get the business 95 percent of the time.
- If you show up on time, with a plan, and implement that plan with excellence . . . you get the business 100 percent of the time!

Make a commitment to show up, on time, with a plan, and then execute your plan with excellence and you will succeed!

A few years ago, my son came home from the College of William and Mary and announced he had achieved honor roll grades for the first time in his two years there. I asked him what the key to his success was, and he said, "Dad, I listened to your tapes and showed up to all my classes, on time!" It is true: if you want to go up, you have got to show up!

10
STEP 3—STAND UP!

If you don't have something you are willing to stand for, you will fall for anything.
—Martin Luther King Jr.

In order to win in life you must stand up and face life—and the challenges it presents—with a determined spirit and a committed mind. I am not talking about physically standing up; I am talking about standing up on the inside. I have friends who are in wheelchairs, unable to physically stand up, yet they are taking life on and they courageously stand up on the inside.

DEVELOP THE LEADER WITHIN

My friend Art Berg, the late speaker and founder of eSpeakers (the online speaker calendar system), was paralyzed in an automobile accident as a young man. But he went on to accomplish incredible things with his life. He was named the Young Entrepreneur of the Year by the Small Business Administration and was named one of *Success* Magazine's Great Comebacks Stories.

Art was confined to a wheelchair, but he consistently stood up on the inside and faced his challenges with courage and a commitment to excellence. (I recommend you get a copy of his book *The Impossible Just Takes a Little Longer* [Harper Paperbacks, 2003]. It will inspire you.) He believed that fate is the hand that you're dealt, but destiny is how you play that hand!

Stand up on the inside and face your problems and your challenges with a determined spirit and a committed mind. You must stand up and be counted—and that takes courage. *Courage* is the "moral, mental, and spiritual strength to take on danger, difficulty, and opposition and to move toward it with determination." Courage does not mean the absence of fear but the willingness to move forward in spite of our fears.

It takes courage to face the challenges of life head-on. Some stick their heads in the ground like an ostrich and hope the challenge will just go away. In reality, it takes courage to face challenges and not give up! And that, my friend, starts with us being honest with ourselves.

In order to live your best life, you must be honest with yourself. And that is hard! I have constantly confronted my own issues and shortcomings and have had to muster the courage to be honest with myself. I realized that the only way I could grow my future and my finances was to get better. The only way I could get better was to be honest with myself and to work on my shortcomings!

When I was younger, I tried to fool myself and make believe that to have high self-esteem I needed to see myself as perfect. As I went through the challenges of life and experienced one setback after another, I was jolted into the reality that to have a better life, I needed to make a commitment to get better. That didn't mean that I didn't love myself or feel good about myself; it meant I loved myself enough to be honest and say that I had room for improvement. Once I caught on to the concept of personal development and lifelong learning, everything changed. And when I changed, things started to change for me!

My life changed when I was willing to be honest with myself and face my own issues. Just as an alcoholic doesn't get better until he realizes that he has a problem, we too only get better when we realize that we need to change. In his book *Just Be Honest* (JMG Publishing, 2002), Steven Gaffney writes, "The worst lies you ever tell are the lies you tell yourself."

One of the biggest challenges to success is the challenge to overcome the enemy within—the enemy we see in the mirror every day.

Just like the Michael Jackson song "Man in the Mirror" says, we have to start with the person we see reflected in the mirror each day. If we are going to be the best we can be, we must start with ourselves. We must be willing to change our ways and make a commitment to get better and to grow—personally and professionally. And in order to change, we must have the courage to be honest with ourselves. We must be willing to confront our self-limiting beliefs and the behaviors that keep us from living our best lives.

HURTS, HABITS, HANG-UPS

We all have past hurts, habits, and hang-ups that impact what we will attempt and what we will pursue. Until we recognize and address them, we will not be able to effectively move forward. Make no mistake: our hurts, habits, and hang-ups can, and will, hold us back. In fact, these issues often keep us in a state of fear and apprehension. In this section I want to look more closely at how to handle our hurts, our habits, and our hang-ups so we can cut the fetters that keep us from soaring as high as we were meant to soar.

Hurts

Past hurts fill us with fear and keep us from even giving our dreams a chance. Past hurts make us give up without even trying. There is the story of the little boy who smelled the hot cherry pie his mother had made and put on top of the stove to cool. He wanted to sneak a piece of the pie so he grabbed the pan—and burned his hand! He burned his hand and never forgot the hurt, so he never touched another cherry pie, hot or cold. He missed out on good cherry pie because of a past hurt.

Sometimes the hurts come from people you love and trust; their negative thinking can alter your life forever. Many people have great talents and abilities but do nothing with them because someone in their past has hurt them with negative words or actions.

It reminds me of the time I gave a speech in Columbus, Ohio, at the Hyatt Hotel. A few hours before the program began, I went to run a sound check, and I met the gentleman preparing to sing the national anthem. He started to warm up and sing a few scales, and I realized that he had a beautiful voice. I knew I was going to get a blessing by hearing him sing that evening. Yet as he started to rehearse, a woman who was mopping the floor hollered to another woman, "Hey, Marge, did you get the name of the cat that died?" and she broke out laughing.

I looked at that woman in total amazement and said, "How can you be so negative?" Fortunately, the singer had not heard her comment.

She said, "Oh, I was just playing." Even though she thought it was harmless fun, it was not. Sticks and stones can break our bones, but words can break our spirits! Those are the same kind of jokes that negative parents say to their children. Sadly, such jokes have a lifelong impact on the self-esteem and—eventually—the achievement of their children.

Just think: If Whitney Houston, Marian Anderson, or Aretha Franklin had been given negative feedback from someone who was "just having some fun," it might have influenced them to never sing again. Not only would their lives have been drastically different, so would ours, and we would be poorer because of it. Be careful with your words, to others and to yourself. If you hear them enough, you, too, can stumble through life thinking you were born to lose, when in reality you were born to *win*!

Habits

We have habits that we know are bad for us, yet we continue to repeat them because we are not willing to change. We are not willing to go through the struggle and discipline of change. We are not willing to face the habits and confront the pain that it will take to change! One example from my life is the bad habit I had for many years of being late. I would always put too much on my schedule, and as a result, I would end up cutting it much too close or being late. One day, I arrived late for a scheduled radio session. The engineer told me he had cancelled a paid date to get me in and that my lateness had cost him a very important client. I was so embarrassed and pained by the expression on his face that I realized I had to change that habit. And I did!

Do you have some bad habits that are impacting your life? Are there some habits that are hurting you or hurting others you care about? If so, change them!

Hang-ups

Finally, we have hang-ups that continuously pull us back. The hang-ups act like an invisible elastic band around our waists that pull us back every time we take a few steps forward. Every time we try to get going and get moving, the hang-ups appear. Like a rubber band, they snap us back to our original positions. We are moving and active, but we are not getting anywhere. To succeed we must have the courage to face the enemies within so we can make the changes to get better. Only then can we do more, be more, and achieve more!

When I was a child, my brother and I would wrestle and tussle with each other, so our parents decided to get us one of those punching bags with the weighted base and the big smiling face. When you hit the bag it would go down temporarily, but it would quickly bounce back up. We would hit that bag every day, and we did everything we could to try to knock the bag down and keep it down, but it would keep bouncing right back up, taunting us with that big smiling face.

We eventually got bored with the bag and left it alone and went looking for other trouble to get into (and my parents would typically reward our efforts with a spanking). Yet every now and then, we would revisit the bag. We would sneak up from behind and in unison we would hit it with everything we had. But it would always bounce back up. And it always had that same big smiling face!

There is a life lesson in this. Life will hit you and occasionally knock you down. But you must bounce back up, and keep bouncing back up. And always keep that big smile on your face! Eventually, life will get bored with you. But then, when you least need it or expect it, life will sneak up on your blind side and hit you with everything it has. That is when it is necessary to go deep within and pull up all the strength you have and look life in the eye and say, "You can knock me down but you will never keep me down, because I am a comeback kid!"

Every now and then, if you are willing to stand up to life and keep fighting for your dream, life will recognize that you are absolutely serious about your success and will leave you alone to find a wimp that will quickly give up and give in. Again, keep fighting for your dreams. It might not happen as quickly as you like, but to those who persist, amazing results can come your way!

Scripture tells of a person who comes to a neighbor's house about midnight and knocks on the door to ask for some bread for friends who have come to visit. The neighbor had gone to bed but reluctantly comes to the window and says that he and his family have gone to bed for the night and the person should come back in the morning. The person keeps knocking and knocking and knocking. Eventually, the neighbor comes to the door and gives the person the bread. The Bible states that the neighbor gave the person bread not because of their friendship but rather because of his importunity, which means persistence. You must persist if you are going to win in life and in business.

Success does not always come when you want it, and therefore you must persist. Case in point: During my second year in the speaking business, Les Brown, "The Motivator," nominated me for the Motivational Speaker Hall of Fame that I mentioned earlier in the book. I did not win. I was nominated the next year, the next, and the next—but I did not win!

Man, did I have to fight discouragement.

Discouragement, by definition, is when we lose heart and lose our courage to keep trying. To get bitter or to get better were my only options. Each failure forced me to continue to get better and stay positive in the process. When we have a problem, it is not so much the problem we face, but the decision we must make. Do we get bitter or get *better*?

Making a commitment to work on myself and to do whatever was necessary to grow into the type of person who was worthy of such an honor became my goal. Getting up earlier. Staying up later. Reading more. Studying more. Each time I did not get the award, I worked even harder on myself.

Finally, after years of hard work, I was inducted into the Motivational Speaker Hall of Fame, and the lesson I learned was that the real gift was in going through the process of growing myself! The real honor came in the lessons I learned along the way. Sometimes, the biggest benefit of reaching your goals is not just hitting the goal but what you become in the process of trying to hit the goal!

MURPHY'S LAW

As you start out after your goals and dreams, watch out, because old Murphy will come and visit. Murphy's Law says that stuff will happen to discourage you and throw you off course at the worse possible moment. My story in *Chicken Soup for the Christian Soul: Stories of Faith: Inspirational Stories of Hope, Devotion, Faith and Miracles* (Chicken Soup for the Soul, 2008) documents my experiences of losing my mother, my brother (who was my only sibling), and my father-in-law (who was my mentor and surrogate father) in the span of twenty-five days. It was a devastating period.

How did I get through that period? This was a time when I had to rely on my faith and my attitude to keep me from losing my mind. I had to decide whether I would curse because the rosebush had thorns or celebrate because the thorn bush had roses. I had to decide whether I would curse because my beloved family members were gone or celebrate that they had come my way. I decided to celebrate!

I followed these three basic guidelines to get through the tough times:

1. Seek help from your family, your friends, and your faith! Also, don't be afraid to get grief counseling. See counseling as an asset, not a liability. If you broke your arm, what would you do? You would go to the doctor! Yet many people have broken hearts and refuse to go get professional help. They try to heal it themselves. Counseling does not make you weak; it helps to keep you strong.

2. Talk to yourself and say, "Life does not have to be perfect to be wonderful!" Ask yourself this question: Do I curse because a rosebush has thorns, or do I celebrate because a thorn bush has roses? Do I curse because the person or situation is no longer the same? Or do I celebrate because that person or that situation came my way?

3. Follow the mantra by Maya Angelou: "If there is something in life you do not like . . . change it! But if you cannot change it, change your attitude!" Decide to have a positive attitude. Abraham Lincoln said, "Most people are about as happy as they choose to be." Choose to be happy. Choose an attitude of gratitude.

What would you do today if you were serious about changing? Make a list of five important items you will undertake. Once you've written down your answer to that question . . . GET BUSY!

11

STEP 4—STEP UP!

The fourth step to five-star success is to step up. You must step up to the plate in life and give it your best shot!

STEP UP TO THE PLATE AND SWING FOR THE FENCES

To have great success, you must consistently swing for the fences. In my new book, *Stop Playing Small: If You Want to Win Big You Must Play Big!* I outline seven steps for big success:

1. Stop playing small . . . Start small, but always think big and play bigger than you think you can!

2. Stop making excuses . . . Start taking action.

3. Stop being a wimp . . . Start being a winner.

4. Stop worrying . . . Start using your faith to succeed.

5. Stop waiting for your ship to come in . . . Start swimming out to it.

6. Stop waiting for God to drop stuff in your lap . . . Start putting your lap where God is dropping stuff.

7. Stop just talking about what you want to do . . . Start doing what you want to do, then talk about it!

Mark Sanborn, author of the bestselling book *The Fred Factor* (Broadway Business, 2004), says: "One of the keys to greater personal and professional success is to remember the 'ABCD principle,' which means to always stay focused on going Above and Beyond the Call of Duty! In terms of job descriptions, some say, 'That is not my job!' Winners say, 'It's all my job! Whatever needs to be done to get the job done is my job!'"

Every day, you must step up and give your best shot, with the understanding that sometimes you will fail. But keep swinging for the fences! Keep giving it your all. Statistics show that the great home run hitters in baseball usually strike out more than they succeed—yet, they keep swinging for the fences. Hank Aaron had twice as many strikeouts as he had home runs. But every time he stepped to the plate he gave it his all. Sometimes he missed, but when he hit it, he knocked it out of the park. When you get your chance to do what you do, make a commitment to give it your best shot. Sometimes you will miss . . . but when you hit it, you will knock it out of the park!

Winners are willing to fail in order to succeed. Many simply do not win because their fear of failure is stronger than their desire for success. People will not bring new ideas to the table because they are afraid of being humiliated if the ideas fail. Or they stay with the old way that has had only moderate success, rather than trying something new that could bring massive success. I know it can be frightening, but I encourage you to face your fears and pursue your dreams.

Failure is painful, but not final—unless you choose for it to be final. On the other hand, nothing is more painful than regret; to look back over your life and wonder what could have been if you had just had the courage to give it a shot!

There is a story about the man who was lying on his deathbed surrounded by ghoulish creatures with bulging eyes and hideous voices. They spoke to him with anger, shouting: "We are the dreams that were given to you to bring to life, yet because of your fear and lack of faith you never gave us a chance. So we must now die with you! How dare you!"

Have courage and swing for the fences. You might miss, but failure is not final, though regret can be! Courage is not the absence of fear; it is having fear and moving forward anyway.

When a batter stands at the plate to swing for the fence, occasionally the pitcher will throw a curve ball. This ball is a pitch that looks like it is perfect to hit, yet at the last moment it takes a strange twist. Life may throw you some curve balls, too. Curve balls are disruptions that try to stall your progress. You will experience a setback, a twist of fate that will throw you off track and distract you from your goal. But don't let the curve balls stop you; learn the strategies for turning the curve ball into a grand slam home run!

Many baseball players have said that the way to hit a curve ball is to keep your eye on the ball, step up, step in, and give it your best shot. Give it your all! I recommend the same strategy in succeeding against life's curve balls. Keep your eye on the goal. Step up to the challenge. Step in and give it your best shot!

WINNERS AREN'T QUITTERS

The old poem "Don't Quit" by Edgar A. Guest is quite accurate in describing how you must keep swinging for the fences, even in the midst of the toughest times. It is as simple as that . . . you must not quit! We must learn strategies for handling the changes and challenges of life. Tough times do not last, but tough people do. You must not just *go* through these tough times. You must *grow* through tough times.

A few years ago I tore ligaments in my foot while playing tennis, and it was both a challenging situation and a great opportunity to learn and grow. As I reflected on the situation, I realized that some of our greatest setbacks are also some of the best training ground for creating a winner's mind-set!

What do you do when you have started out on your goals and dreams and calamity strikes? I say, first you must decide to keep your eye on the prize and not on the problems! Problems in life will come. In fact, it is through the problems and pains of life that we grow . . . that is why we call them "growing pains." Yet, we must decide whether we will *go* through the problems or *grow* through the problems! That decision will determine our actions, and our actions will determine our results.

Sometimes life will knock you down—and try to knock you out! Yet I encourage you to pick yourself up, dust yourself off, catch your breath, and get moving again in the direction of your goals.

A few years ago, I heard the story of a marathon runner who went to war and was involved in a mortar accident. As a result, he lost his lower body. In fact, he lost so much of his lower body that prosthetic legs were not possible. He was down, but he made up his mind that he was not out. When he recovered from his injuries, he told the doctors that the first thing he wanted to do was to start training for another marathon. They reminded him that he had no legs and that it would be almost impossible to move around without a wheelchair. Any movement he made without the use of his wheelchair would require him to use his hands and arms to swing his body from spot to spot.

He thanked the doctors for their concern, but he had made up his mind that he was going to run another marathon . . . without a wheelchair!

He started working on his goal; he practiced for months just swinging his body from spot to spot and moving around his house. Then he started working on going farther. He trained for almost a year and was finally able to swing himself a mile! He kept on training and got up to two miles, then three miles, and then four miles. He continued to train until he felt he was ready to try twenty-six miles! He started the race with all the other able-bodied racers. The others all finished that same day, some in a few hours, but not him. It took him two days of non-stop swinging of his body from one spot to another.

When he finally crossed the finish line, the only people there were his family and a single newspaper reporter. As he crossed the finish line, with his hands bloodied and his leg stumps raw, the newspaper reporter could not believe this man had continued, considering the intense pain he must have been experiencing! As his family members prepared to take him to the hospital, the reporter asked how it was that the pain did not stop him. The marathoner replied: "Yes, it was painful! But every time the pain became intense, I would focus my energy on the goal, and I would think about how I would feel crossing the finish line. The joy I would get from achieving the prize was more powerful than the pain of the problem!"

I want you to know you will have some challenges in your quest for success, but please do not stop. Do not give up! Do not let those challenges derail your success. Focus on the prize of achieving your goal rather than on the pain of the problem. If you do, you will see that in time your prizes will grow and your problems will shrink, and most of all you will Grow Yourself and Grow Your Success!

Through the physical challenge of my torn ligaments, I learned firsthand that my friend W Mitchell, the award-winning inspirational speaker who survived two life-altering accidents and refused to give up on his dreams, is absolutely right. W Mitchell has become known as the man who was burned in a motorcycle crash and then paralyzed in an airplane accident yet shares with people around the world that it doesn't matter what happens to you, it's what you do about it that counts! I truly believe that a setback is nothing but a setup for a comeback, and I am a comeback kid! How about you?

I love the quote by Jim Rhone that states, "Don't pray that the problem were smaller, pray that you were bigger! Don't pray that the situation was easier, pray that you were bigger! Don't pray that God would move the mountain, pray that God would make you stronger to overcome the mountains in your life! Pray that you become bigger, better an stronger!" In every challenge there is an opportunity, if you are willing to think differently and work on creating new opportunities. Don't just look at it as a problem, but rather think of it as a decision that must be made for your future! I encourage you to be willing to change your perspective about the challenges you face, and see them as opportunities to grow rather than situations that you are going through.

I believe that the best way to predict the future is to create the future. So, get up, get dreaming, get going, get stretching, and get busy really living life at another level!

Use the changes and challenges of life to propel you to that next level. Remember that in chapter 3 I recommended the Three C's for Success: Change, Challenge, and Choices regarding change management in your professional life? Let's apply them now to your personal life.

CHANGE

Someone once said that the only constant in life is change. Change is a part of the success process, but it takes work to get through the process.

Change is constant and uncomfortable. We do not want to change! No matter how many books we read or seminars we attend in regard to "embracing change," it is still uncomfortable. It is uncomfortable because we are creatures of habit and we tend to do what we have always done. Yet we must change if we want to grow.

Try this exercise: Stop, cross your arms, and look at which arm is on top. (Put the book down for a minute and cross those arms!) Now that you have found which one is on top, do it again, and this time switch your arms. Do you notice how uncomfortable it is? The reason it is so uncomfortable is that you have been crossing your arms the same way since before you were born! Babies start crossing their arms in their mother's womb, and they never change the arm that rests on top. We are creatures of habit, and therefore it is very, very uncomfortable to change. Yet change is necessary for growth, so we have to work on the habits that keep us from growing and succeeding at the highest levels.

As a full-time nightclub singer, I sang the song "Everything Must Change!" just about every night, but I never noticed how profound the words were. Years later, I realized I'd been singing about a great truth. Everything really does change. In fact, everything *must* change, and only those who are quickest to embrace and adapt to change win at the highest levels.

All progress is the result of change. Everything you are experiencing at this moment is the result of change. This book is the result of change. A room lit by lightbulbs rather than candles is the result of change. If you are reading this book on a computer as an e-book, then that is a result of change. If you are listening to the audio version of this book on CD or seeing my message on DVD or video, then that is the result of change. There was a time when there were no computers, no CDs, and no DVDs or videos. All of this progress is the result of CHANGE! Can you see why, then, we should see change as an ally, not as an enemy? In doing so, we can live a better life!

If you have children, you will remember how, when they were babies, they would move about by crawling. And one day, miraculously, they stood on their own two feet for the very first time. They weebled and wobbled, and typically, they fell down. But no parent ever said, "Stay down, baby!" Instead, they said: "Get up! Try again! Come to Mommy! Come to Daddy! Try again!" The baby usually tries again and falls down again, but it keeps trying and trying until it learns to stay up. Babies take the first step, then the second step, and then the third. When the baby falls down, sometimes it falls on its backside, but sometimes it falls on its face! But the parent doesn't stop the baby from falling and trying. Moms and dads encourage their babies to try again, and again, and again.

Parents know that if the baby does not fall and get back up, it will never learn to walk. And if the baby does not fall and get back up, it will never learn to run. If the baby does not fall and get back up, it will never learn to maximize its ability. Yet many people who fail in their attempts to achieve a goal get discouraged and give up. In doing so, they short-circuit their long-term success and long-term possibilities.

See change as a struggle that is worth the effort.

CHALLENGE

The second of the Three C's for Success is challenge. Challenge is going to happen in life. What is a challenge? It is something that tests your resolve and determination to push forward in spite of the obstacles. That something might have been a personal or a professional setback.

The setback does not have to be the end of the road, however; it can be a bend in the road. And when it is a bend in the road, you can change and go in another direction. In fact, the only ones who crash and burn are those who fail to change, like Wylie Coyote in the Coyote-Road Runner cartoon series, who would not change his path and inevitably would run into the side of the mountain! We must learn to navigate the winds of change and go with the changes in the road as we move along in life.

Our challenges, like everything else in life, are affected by Murphy's Law, which says, "Anything that can go wrong will go wrong." And I would add, "at the worst possible time!" Marlon Brando once said, "The Messenger of Misery [that is, Murphy] comes to visit everyone!" Murphy has your name, address, and telephone number on a piece of paper and is coming to visit you sooner or later. A gentleman came up to me after a program and said that Murphy didn't just come to visit him; Murphy had a room at his house! I laughed out loud.

CHOICES

Finally, after facing change and challenge, we come face to face with the last of the Three *C*'s for Success—choices! Success in life ultimately comes down to your choices. My friend Marlon Smith, the high-tech motivator and president of Success by Choice, is known for telling audiences that your "success is your choice." Success truly is a choice and not a chance. You must choose to succeed. You choose to sleep in, or you choose to get up and get busy. You choose to think big, or you choose to think small. You choose to be positive, or you choose to be negative. You choose to keep fighting for your dreams, or you choose to give in.

We all have experiences we cannot control, and so we must make choices. We cannot choose what life throws at us, but we can choose how we respond to what life throws at us. Or as I like to say in speeches, we cannot control what happens to us or what happens around us, but we have complete control over what happens *in* us! Choose to have a positive outlook, a positive in-look, and a positive up-look.

STEP IT UP TO THE NEXT LEVEL

After you step up to the plate and give it your best shot, you must step it up, which means to step up your game and play at another level! Find a way to consistently and continually better your best! My speech today is better than yesterday's speech, but tomorrow's speech is going to be better than today's.

Why? After today's speech I am going to go and work on my message and improve it. I have a great desire to get better! I cannot forget the bridge that brought me across to all that I've achieved—the bridge called "Better" that changed my business. It was making the commitment to get better and to look for ways to create constant and never-ending improvement that helped me grow as a speaker and as a person. It was the lessons I learned about making a commitment to a never-ending pursuit of excellence that helped me grow.

Make a commitment to personal development. Make a commitment to read one self-help or personal development book a month from here on out. As long as you have life, keep working on getting better. Learn a new language or a new skill, or take courses to take your present skills to another level. Not only does it make you better, but studies show that learning new languages and new skills strengthens your brain and helps prevent and offset Alzheimer's disease. Whatever the reason you decide to make the commitment, I can tell you that when you change, things will change for you!

Change, challenge, and choices are a part of the personal development program for winners. Stand up to life, stand up to yourself, and stand up to changes and challenges of life and declare: "I am a winner, and winners never quit and quitters never win! I am a winner!"

12

STEP 5—THINK UP!

When I say, "think up," I literally mean that I want you to think "up" thoughts even in "down" times. To think up is to think about your possibilities and not get stuck thinking about the probabilities. Probability thinking would say that a former nightclub singer who got fired and was broke, busted, and disgusted would have very little chance to have a successful career as a professional speaker. Yet possibility thinking said: "Willie, give it a shot! You have always had a desire to inspire! Plus, you should never let your present circumstances determine your future possibilities! Go for it! Everything's possible!" I decided to focus on possibilities.

Next, to think up means to be a forward thinker, one who anticipates the needs of others and plans and prepares for the future. To be a forward thinker is to be like the ant, one of the most productive creatures on the face of the Earth. Ants prepare for the winter while it is still summer. They do not let winter catch them without supplies to survive. They think about winter all summer long.

To be a forward thinker is to have forethought about the goals that you are trying to reach. It also involves being proactive about what needs to be done, rather than waiting for someone to tell you what to do. When hiring new staff, I always look for people who are forward thinkers; people who do not need to be told daily what they should do but rather think ahead and come up with ideas on how to reach our goals faster. Start planning and preparing and thinking about tomorrow today!

To think up is to think beyond the ordinary and think extraordinary. We've all heard the popular phrase "Think outside the box." Nido Qubein, president of High Point University and a business growth expert, however, says we should not stop there. "We should throw the box completely out! And learn to think beyond the confines of any box we might be in."

Always seek ways to grow your success with new ideas and strategies to reach your goals! For example, I was once booked in two different cities on the same day: one in Florida and the other in Maryland. There were no flights available to get me from one event to the next in the appropriate time frame. We could not change the time for either event, and chartering a private jet was too expensive.

Then I started thinking outside the box. I asked the client in Maryland if it would be okay for me to be there, yet not be there *physically*.

He said, "Well, yeah!"

I suggested a "live" television transmission to his group from the city I was in, in Florida. He loved the idea! I spoke from a television studio in Orlando. Then I headed across town to my other client in that city.

In his landmark book *Think and Grow Rich* (Aventine Press, original version restored and revised by author, 2004), Napoleon Hill wrote, "Whatever the mind of man can conceive and believe it can achieve!" Earl Nightingale says that the reason most people don't succeed in life is not because of a lack of talent or ability, it's because they simply don't think! There's a verse from the Book of Proverbs that says, "As a man thinketh in his heart, so he is!" In order to live a five-star life and have a five-star organization, we must make a commitment to Think Up! Think about the possibilities and create a plan to make your dreams come true.

One of the most effective techniques to get to the five-star lifestyle is to start with the end in mind. The end, the goal, is clearly placed in your mind, and then you start to think about how to most effectively reach that destination. Imagine starting on a long trip without taking time to map out your path. You would get into your car and start driving without planning your route. That would be the makings of a disaster!

MAKE UP YOUR MIND TO W.I.N.

In chapter 5, I mentioned that it is very important to make up your mind to W.I.N., which was a focus on doing *whatever is necessary* to please your customers. Now I want to apply that same discussion to your personal success, with a focus on you winning more of the challenges in life. As I stated earlier, I believe that in the quest for success, there is nothing more powerful than a made-up mind! When you make up your mind that you are going to definitely achieve your goal and you will not allow anything to stop you, you get amazing power.

I mentioned earlier that the ant is one of God's most incredible creatures. The ant is a forward thinker and prepares for winter all summer, but that is not all that is amazing about the ant. The ant has a made-up mind-set, a winner's mind-set. Ants achieve their goal—or else. If you put a piece of bread in front of an ant and then place a row of bricks between the ant and the bread, the ant will do whatever is necessary to get to that bread. It will go around the bricks, or it will go over the bricks, or it will dig under the bricks, but it will get to the bread. You can rest assured that the problem is that most people do not make up their minds in such a definitive manner. Most people say they want to achieve their goals, but very few are actually committed to achieving their goals. I say you should stretch and go big!

To get a winner's mind-set you must be willing to keep going in spite of the obstacles. Make up your mind and commit to achieve your goals without any trepidation or hesitation. When you do this, you tend to win more. Singers . . . sing, dancers . . . dance, runners . . . run, and winners . . . win! Winners find a way to win. They are not sure how they are going to win, they just find a way to make it happen. Joe Montana, the famous quarterback, developed his reputation as a player who always found a way to win. Michael Jordan, considered the greatest "winner" in the history of basketball, made a habit of finding a way to win.

Magic Johnson, the basketball star-turned-entrepreneur, developed a winner's attitude as a youngster, and it has helped him achieve amazing results. When he was in high school, he led his team to a state championship. When he was in college, he led his team to a national championship. When he entered the ranks of professional basketball, he led his team to an NBA championship! When he was infected with the HIV virus, many thought his days were numbered. But again, his winner's attitude helped him win against impossible odds. While fighting to build and protect his health, he entered the business ranks and won again. He has become one of America's most prolific entrepreneurs, with Magic Johnson theaters, restaurants, Starbucks coffee shops, and housing developments. Magic Johnson proves again that winners win. He has successfully lived with the HIV virus for more than fifteen years.

Winners don't always know how they are going to win; they just expect to win, and they find a way to win over and over again! Even against impossible odds, they find a way to win. When we think of winning we usually think about those who are first or best in a contest, but that is not the totality of winning. Winning is also about overcoming our own self-limitations in order to reach a goal. Booker T. Washington said, "Greatness is not about what you achieve in life, but rather what you must overcome in order to achieve it!"

Winning is more than just crossing the finish line first. It is making a personal commitment to fight through the challenges in order to achieve a goal. It is about gaining possession by exerting great effort! And most times, putting forth your greatest effort happens when you overcome your self-limiting beliefs. After being the first person to successfully climb Mount Everest, Sir Edmund Hillary said, "It is not the mountain we conquered, it is ourselves!" He said he had to overcome his doubts, fears, hesitancy, and thoughts of quitting in order to achieve his goal.

It takes great effort to win in life, and the reason most people do not win is because they are unable to exert enough consistent effort. Many people start out with real sincerity to achieve their goals and work real hard . . . for a while. But then the challenges come and they fall off. They cannot sustain the effort and therefore don't win.

What can change this pattern? What can help people have greater success in their personal and professional endeavors? What can help people to sustain and maintain the momentum to actually have a string of winning moments? It is the development of a winner's attitude. It is a commitment to develop the will to win!

How do you get that winner's attitude? First, start by telling yourself you are a winner! Look in the mirror and tell yourself that you were born for greatness. Repeat that every time you look in the mirror—at least three times a day. Next, make a habit of filling your mind up with the pure, the powerful, and the positive. How do you do this? Read one self-help book a month. When you first wake up, turn off the news for that first twenty minutes of your day and listen, instead, to twenty minutes of positive messages. Refuse to participate in negative conversation. Find five small things daily that you are thankful for. These actions will turn into a reservoir of possibilities! Then think about the great things you want to achieve, and start preparing for them!

There is a story about a man who talked about owning a Bentley, which he had seen at an auto show one day. He got pictures of the Bentley and hung them in his bedroom. He looked at the pictures every day. Then he lost his job and decided to start his own company, which he ran out of his spare bedroom. One day he went out to the garage and cleaned it out. When his family asked him why, he said, "Because that is where my Bentley is going to go!" They laughed and told him he had lost his mind, because he was barely making ends meet with his new company. But he didn't laugh, he just kept working on himself and his business and preparing for the day he could park his Bentley in the garage.

He would go to the library every morning to read and study, then he would go to the garage every evening to clean the spot where his Bentley would go. Everyone continued to laugh at him, but he worked on himself and worked on his dream—and about two years later, he drove his Bentley into the parking space in his garage!

On my desk I keep a sign that reads, "Winners make things happen and losers let things happen!" Another way of saying this is: "Some people make things happen, others watch what happened, and the rest of us stand around and ask, 'What happened?'" Whatever way you want to say it, the truth remains that those who are winners are those who make a determined decision to win!

OBSTACLES TO OUR OWN SUCCESS

When asked what keeps them from being a success, most people blame the government or the economy or their families. Some blame the "isms" of life: you know, sexism, racism, ageism, and so forth. But the one thing that most people avoid putting on their blame list is the most important factor—themselves! We are the main obstacles to our success in life.

It has been said that success follows the 80-20 rule. In a corporate setting, the 80-20 dynamic says that 80 percent of the work usually comes from 20 percent of the people. In personal achievement, you can look at it this way: we are responsible for 80 percent of our failure to hit our goals, and outside obstacles are only 20 percent of the problem. Or as Pogo said, "We have found the enemy and he is us!" We must be brutally honest and come to the realization that we are the biggest challenge to our own success! If you want to win, you must stop *letting* things happen and start *making* things happen! Remember, when all is said and done, it is still up to you.

DECIDE TO WIN/REFUSE TO LOSE

I recently took a twenty-three-hour flight to Japan. I had planned to write a couple of chapters for my new book during that time. I even bought a heavy-duty, long-lasting battery for my laptop. After boarding the flight, I settled in my seat, ready to get to work. I pressed the power button on the computer, eagerly waiting for the screen to light up—but nothing happened! The computer would not come on. I tried and tried and tried again, but nothing happened. I soon realized that the problem was with the screen; the screen was broken and the computer simply was not going to work.

At this point, I was not only disappointed but also really frustrated. But I knew I had a decision to make. I remembered a quote I'd learned years ago: "When things go wrong and you are faced with great challenges, you don't have just a problem to deal with, you have a decision to make." So I made the decision to move on to Plan B. I typed the chapters on my cell phone! The keyboard was small and my fingers were cramped, but I got the job done!

Things will always attempt to distract and disrupt you from accomplishing your goals. When these challenges appear in your life, remember: it's not just a problem you need to deal with, it's a decision you have to make. Decide to win, refuse to lose, and move forward in spite of the challenges.

What challenges are stopping you? What issues have kept you from accomplishing your goals? And most important, what are you going to do about it? I encourage you to keep learning, keep striving, and never give up! Don't let the challenges keep you from reaching your goals. Decide to win, refuse to lose—and keep striving!

It starts with a winner's attitude, which includes a made-up mind. A made-up mind is a mind that says, "I am going to win!" It also includes an expectation that this is going to happen some how, some way. I encourage you to make up your mind to win.

Try this exercise. Stand up. Turn your body as far as you absolutely can to the right. (Do it now. I'll wait for you!) Now that you have gone as far as you absolutely can to the right, I want you to do it again and this time try to go even further. (I'll wait again. For you, I would be willing to wait all day). Did you notice how much further you went when you pushed it? The same is true for your goals and dreams! That said, I have some important homework for you to do.

Imagine you went to the doctor today and were told that you have a rare illness. This illness guarantees you will be dead a year from now. But it also guarantees that anything you attempt, anything you try, you will achieve! What ten things would you attempt if you knew you could not fail? Write those ten things down on a piece of paper. Think as big as you can and dream as big as you can. Go as far as you can, and once you get there you will see that you can go even farther! What do you have to fear, and what do you have to lose? Give it a shot!

THE POWER OF SETTING GOALS

Do you want massive success? Do you want huge results? In my first book, *It Only Takes a Minute to Change Your Life!*, I wrote about Arnold Schwarzenegger, who is now the governor of California. Governor Schwarzenegger discovered some of the secrets to *massive success*, and you can use those same tips to help make your dreams come true.

Although he left Austria with only a few possessions, he left with something more important than money and things—a dream and the determination to make that dream become a reality. He wrote his dream down on an index card that he called his "personal contract"—a contract he made with himself.

On the card he handwrote his four goals. Arnold read it daily and made a vow to himself that he would make those goals into realities. The four goals were: (1) to become the greatest bodybuilder of all time; (2) to become a wealthy movie star; (3) to marry into a prestigious family; and (4) to become successful in politics!

Arnold Schwarzenegger became the youngest person to receive the Mr. Universe title. He won the Mr. Olympia title seven times before retiring to begin a career making movies. Arnold Schwarzenegger's first movie featured him as a bodybuilder, but he continued to grow his acting skills. In time, he became one of the highest paid movie stars in the business.

Arnold's third goal was to marry well, and he did! He married into the prestigious Kennedy family. And he made a commitment to become politically active, first by becoming the chairman of the President's Committee on Physical Fitness and then by becoming active in the National Republican Party. Yet he still knew there were bigger fish to fry and bigger achievements to accomplish. He re-read his "personal contract" and realized that his goal was to become *successful* in politics. He set out to accomplish that goal, and he did it! In November 2003 Arnold Schwarzenegger was elected governor of California.

In the process of achieving success in America, Schwarzenegger learned how clear goals and a commitment to those goals can transform your life, your finances, and your future. He learned how to make his goals into realities and developed the confidence necessary to make that happen. Governor Schwarzenegger has shown that there is power in setting goals, and those who learn how to set clear goals and make a commitment to achieving those goals are the ones who will achieve incredible results!

He gives us more than a clear example of the power of goals. He also provides a clear example of the mind-set of winners. Winners . . . win! They have a winner's mind-set and a winner's attitude and they expect to win. We can learn the secrets to long-term success from Arnold Schwarzenegger. First, have a vision. Second, set goals. Third, make a commitment to those goals. Fourth, make a commitment to your commitments. Fifth, and finally, never give up!

If you are willing to dream big and go out and do the necessary work to turn your goals into realities, then you too can do what others call impossible! Let us all learn from Schwarzenegger: there is power in setting goals. Scripture says, "Write the vision, and make it plain, that he that reads it may run the race!" Write your goals and make them clear and focused. Then get busy going about the business of achieving those goals. If you do, then in time you too can be like Arnold Schwarzenegger. You can start to make history and do those things that others say is impossible . . . and in the process you can start to actually live your dreams!

Goals versus Commitments

Simon Bailey, the international speaker, author, and "brilliance" expert, says we should have goals, but we should also have commitments. The goals are items we would like to achieve, yet the commitments are the things that we *must* achieve! In an interview with Simon on my XM radio show, he said: "Willie, you have been married for over twenty years. When you got married, did you set a goal to stay married or did you make the commitment? I believe that the reason you have been married for over twenty years is because you made a commitment to stay married, rather than setting a goal to stay married." And you know what? Simon was right!

We set goals to achieve what we would *like* to achieve, but we make commitments to achieve what we *must* achieve! What are your goals and what are your commitments? Stop right now. Write a list of ten things you would like to achieve. Put the heading "Goals: What I want to achieve!" at the top of the page. Then write down ten things that you are *committed* to achieve! Put the heading "Commitments: What I must achieve!" at the top of that page. Do it now!

HOW BADLY DO YOU WANT TO ACHIEVE IT?

I have focused a great deal over the years on the power and impact of desire and the value of asking yourself, "How badly do I want to achieve my goal?" Desire is a critical element in the quest for success. No matter what you attempt, you will always have obstacles and hurdles. It is your desire that ultimately keeps you on track to achieve your goals.

Imagine you come home after a long day of working hard and there is absolutely nothing in the house to eat. What are you going to do? Most people give me the following answers:

Go to the grocery store.

Go to a fast-food restaurant.

Go to a convenience store.

Go to a friend's house.

Further imagine, in response to those answers, that—

The grocery store is closed.

The fast-food restaurant had a power failure and has no food prepared.

The convenience store has not gotten their food shipment in today.

Your friend is not home.

What are you going to do? Try another restaurant or go to another friend's home? If you notice, you did not say you would give up. Why? Because when you are really hungry, you don't even think about giving up!

A "soda at midnight" is an analogy I often share with audiences. You must have great desire and great determination to get a soda at midnight if that's what you want. Many people may say they want it "real bad," but the definitive question is how bad is "real bad" to you?

Imagine that a person wakes up at midnight and says, "I want a soda and I want it real bad!" That person gets up, walks to the refrigerator, but finds no sodas. The person walks to the window, opens the shades, and sees that it's snowing. Then the person checks the refrigerator one more time, still finds no sodas, and settles for a glass of water and goes back to bed because that person really did not want the soda THAT BAD!

A second person wakes up around midnight and says, "I want a soda and I want it real bad!" That person gets up, walks to the refrigerator, but finds no sodas. The second person walks to the window, opens the shades, and sees that it's snowing. Then the second person checks the refrigerator one more time, still finds no sodas, and puts on a coat and gloves and boots and walks to the corner store. But the corner store is closed, so the second person goes back home, settles for a glass of orange juice, and goes back to bed. The second person really did not want the soda THAT BAD!

A third person wakes up around midnight and says, "I want a soda and I really want it real bad!" That person gets up, walks to the refrigerator, but finds no sodas. The third person walks to the window, opens the shades, and sees that it's snowing. The third person then checks the refrigerator one more time, still finds no sodas, and puts on a coat and gloves and boots and walks to the corner store. But the corner store is closed. The third person walks another quarter mile to the all-night market, but due to the snowstorm, it too is closed. The third person then walks another half mile to a gas station with a soda machine, but the sodas are sold out! Yet that person keeps walking and trying, and walking and trying, and walking and trying to get a soda! That person wants it so bad they are willing to keep going until they attain their goal!

I shared that analogy during a radio interview, and the radio show host was quiet for a few seconds. Then he said: "Willie Jolley, that is the most ridiculous thing I have ever heard! Who is going to go out in a blizzard for a soda? That is ridiculous!"

I responded: "You are absolutely right—it *is* ridiculous! See, I have found that only those who attempt the ridiculous are those who achieve the spectacular!"

Oprah Winfrey was told it was ridiculous for a woman who came from her humble beginnings to think she could ever be a major television personality. Yet she attempted the ridiculous and achieved the spectacular! *The Oprah Winfrey Show* has remained the number one talk show for twenty-two consecutive seasons. Bill Gates was a Harvard University dropout. When he said he wanted to see a day where there would be a computer, with his software, in every school and home, he was told it was ridiculous. Yet that is why he is the wealthiest man in the world—he was willing to attempt the ridiculous and achieve the spectacular! He made the computer fast and affordable for the average consumer.

Desire is about your willingness to keep going in spite of the odds. It is about your willingness to do what others consider ridiculous in order to achieve your goals. You must have a winning appetite. How bad do you want it? How bad do you want to W.I.N.?

You must think ridiculous, outrageous thoughts. Then muster the courage to go after those goals and dreams so you too can experience the five-star life.

ARE YOU SERIOUS?

Not long ago I got a note from an old friend of mine from the days when I was singing in nightclubs. He said he had read about my induction into the Motivational Speaker Hall of Fame and had seen me on television and wanted to know what I did to change my life. I told him that I decided to change, and as Jim Rohn says, "Once you change, everything changes for you!" I told him I made a commitment to grow me and to expand my thinking. I started a course of self-development and made a commitment to read positive books, listen to motivational tapes, and attend lots of motivational seminars.

In short, I told him that I decided to "get serious" about my success. I made up my mind that I was going to do whatever was necessary for success. I remember Les Brown telling me once that most people are "seriously not serious about success!" He said they talk about it, and talk about it, and talk about it, but they never do anything about it.

So I made up my mind to get serious! I made a commitment to get up early and stay up late, I made a commitment to read everything I could about self-development, so I turned off the television and invested heavily in books and tapes. I made the commitment to get on the phone and make more sales calls. I would get on the phone early in the morning and would continue until late into the evening, and when I got tired and wanted to stop, I would always make one more call. I made a commitment that on a daily basis I would do more than I was paid to do, and give more than I was expected to give, and go further than I was asked to go.

My friend then asked me what three things I do on a daily basis. I told him that I start each day the same way: with prayer and meditation. I thank God for each new morning that I get out of bed, and I proudly proclaim, "This is the day that the Lord has made and I am glad and rejoice in it!" I have an attitude of gratitude because I have another opportunity to go out and live my dream!

Second, I ask myself, "Willie, what would you do today if you were serious?" I ponder that question, and then I list all of the answers.

Third, I review the list and get busy on achieving those items!

I told my friend that this was not rocket science, but it did take a PHD, which stands for Persistence, Hunger, and Determination! Most of all it takes a commitment to grow ourselves so we can grow our futures. Then we must make a commitment to that commitment! In other words, we must get serious about success! My question to you today is this: "What would you do today if you were serious?"

CONCLUSION

So, these are my simple steps for success, my simple steps for developing a will to win and an Attitude of Excellence! These steps are essential for creating a five-star organization and critical for developing a five-star lifestyle. Some people want a five-star lifestyle and continue to wait for their ship to come in with hopes of hitting the big one! They are waiting for the lottery or for their horse to come in first or for an inheritance, yet they do not realize that they can have everything right now! The minute you decide and move in the new direction of taking these steps to success by incorporating them into your lifestyle, you are on the way. I encourage you to move on these steps today. Do not delay, move right now . . . move today!

The five-star life is not just for movie stars or the rich and famous; it is for all people who decide to grow themselves so they can grow their futures. Remember, the best way to grow your future is to grow yourself, and the best way to grow your organization is to grow your people! Five-star organizations are always looking to hire, acquire, and do whatever is necessary to get the best people working for them. And if they cannot hire them, they will make them! Make the commitment today to get on board and get moving toward your dreams and the five-star lifestyle!

Success is a game, so you might as well play it to win! That is a philosophy that I have come to live my life by, and it has had a profound impact on my thinking and my actions. I want to encourage you to live your life with power and passion and enjoy life to the fullest.

I often hear athletes say that they are giving their all in the pursuit of winning the game and that they will leave it all on the field. Michael Jordan was known to give so much on the basketball court that he barely had enough energy to walk to the dressing room. During one playoff game he played while suffering the effects of the flu. After a superb effort, which included hitting the winning shot, Michael Jordan had to be carried off the court! I have come to find that the great performers in other fields have the same philosophy. They believe that it is important to give their all in their pursuit of excellence, and they leave everything on the field or on the stage or in the boardroom. They play hard and give their all in the pursuit of excellence.

I like to tell audiences that I believe we should live full and die empty, giving our all while here on Earth. My friend Myles Munroe says that the richest place on the Earth is the graveyard, where people take their million-dollar ideas and dreams that they didn't take advantage of while they were living. He calls it a "dying shame!" My mentor Rosita Perez says to make sure that we do not take our music with us to our graves; rather, we should create a life that is a symphony. Live life to the fullest, and when your time comes, leave with an assurance that you did all you could in the time you had to do it!

I believe that God's gift to us is life, and our gift to Him is how we live our lives. How we do and give and make a difference in the world. It is within each of us to take the mantle upon us and live up to the possibilities that are within our grasp. I used to say we should live up to our potential, but I now believe that is also limiting because once we are engaged and energized, we can rise above the perception we have of ourselves and learn to play above our heads. We can learn to play above what we consider to be our own potential. I believe we can achieve incredible results if we believe that we can and then go out and start working on manifesting those beliefs in our realities.

THE BEST IS YET TO COME!

I had an experience years ago that had a tremendous impact on my thinking and my actions, and it continues to encourage and empower me to this day. I was a new speaker and I was struggling with my business. I was struggling to keep the phone on and keep the electric company from turning the lights off. It was tough, and I was hoping that someone would call and book me to speak so I could pay my bills. Finally, I got a call from an organization in Orlando, Florida. They booked me to come and speak for their conference. I was so excited that I was going to make some money that I could hardly contain myself.

I went to Florida and gave the speech, and they gave me a standing ovation. I was on cloud nine! I got my check, and they even enclosed a small bonus for doing a good job. I got on the plane to return home full of excitement because I had gotten paid. But then I started thinking about all my bills and expenses, and I realized that the money was already accounted for. It was allocated to everyone but me! All of a sudden I got depressed because the money was gone before I had a chance to even deposit it in my account.

As I sat there having a pity party with myself, I started talking to an older gentleman across the aisle. He must have sensed that I was struggling, and during the conversation he asked me a question that would have a profound impact on my life. He said, "Young man, how old do you think I am?"

I looked at him and I said, "Well, I would say you are about sixty."

He smiled, took off his glasses, and looked me right in the eyes and said: "Young man, I travel around the country speaking to people about health and wealth, and I do it every day. And I want you to know that I am eighty-eight years old, and my best is yet to come!"

In that moment everything changed for me! If an eighty-eight-year-old man could see that his best days were in front of him and not behind him, what in the world did I have to whine and cry about? If an eighty-eight-year-old man could have that kind of optimism, what was keeping me from my success? The answer was that the problem was me. I was waiting for success to come to me rather than going out and creating success for myself. The answer was that I was the problem and that I had to change my thinking and change my attitude and change my actions. Rather than waiting for people to call me, I needed to call them. Rather than waiting for God to drop things in my lap, I needed to take action and start moving my lap where God was dropping things! As I left the plane that day I was a new person.

I went home with a new attitude and new optimism. I got on the phone and started making sales calls and started to talk to more people about my business, and things started to change. That old gentleman was absolutely right—the best was yet to come!

Many years have gone by since that man spoke those words into my life and encouraged me, and a lot has happened. I have had success as a speaker, success as an author, and success with radio and television, yet I believe that this is just the tip of the iceberg of what is possible. I truly believe the best is yet to come!

As I end this book, I want to remind you that we have covered a lot of ground. In the first part of this book, "The Will to Win: Developing a Culture of Excellence," we talked about developing the leader in you. We talked about seeing change as an ally, not an enemy. We talked about thinking like a team and working like a team so you can win like a team. We talked about giving customer service that is beyond good and beyond great: *Wow* customer service. We talked about how critical your attitude is in this process.

In the second part of this book, "Personal Development: Five Simple Steps for Five-Star Success," we talked about how you must *Wake Up and Dream* and consider the possibilities, not the probabilities. We talked about how you must *Show Up* and do more than you are expected to do and give more than you are expected to give . . . with an understanding that if you do more than you are paid to do, you will in time be paid more than you do! We talked about how you must *Stand Up* and face life's challenges with a determination that will grow you and grow your success. We talked about how your must *Step Up* to the plate and give your best shot. How you must keep swinging for the fence and not let the fear of failure stop you! Finally, we talked about how you must *Think Up* and *make up your mind to W.I.N.!* Think "up" thoughts, even in down times. Keep the faith and keep a positive attitude—a *winner's* attitude.

I have pressed these points on you because I have a secret: *YOUR BEST IS YET TO COME!* These points will be the road signs to lead you to the place where you can become your best you! I am excited for you, and I hope to hear from you about the tremendous things that have happened in your life. I look back to the day I met that eighty-eight-year-old man who encouraged me that my best was yet to come if I would just believe and proceed and become the best me I could be! I wish I could find him and let him know how much his words meant. I hope that one day I will meet you and you can tell me if his words have helped you as much as they helped me. In the meantime, go forth and live your life with passion, and make sure you share this information with others. Let them know that no matter where they are at this present time, their best is yet to come! God bless you!

WILLIE JOLLEY'S BESTSELLING SUCCESS PRODUCTS

A Setback Is a Setup for a Comeback
Willie Jolley's international bestseller *A Setback Is a Setup for a Comeback* takes these words of wisdom and creates a fun-filled educational book of how to overcome, achieve, and believe. This impactful page-turner provides inspiration and motivation to all who read it.

"If you ever find yourself in a low place, this book will help show you the way up, the way out, and the way beyond! A magnificent read!" —Les Brown, bestselling author of *Live Your Dreams*

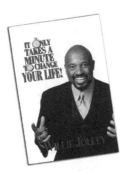

It Only Takes a Minute to Change Your Life
Willie Jolley's national bestseller *It Only Takes a Minute to Change Your Life* is an inspirational and motivational book that will show you how to release the power within you. This fast-paced book provides readers with over 150 of Willie Jolley's magnificent motivational "one minute messages" that help readers do more, be more, and achieve more.

"Willie Jolley takes us for the ride of our lives, to the heart of success and achievement!" —Dr. Dennis Kimbro, bestselling author of *What Makes the Great Great!*"

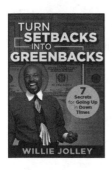

Turn Setbacks into Greenbacks
Willie Jolley's latest book is destined to be a self-help classic. He shares seven fundamental steps that will help you turn tough times into wealth-building times. This book should be a key tool in building your financial freedom!

"A wonderful book . . . When you open it, you'll feel the vitality of unrealized choices, and when you close it, you'll feel energized to change your life for your own benefit and for those around you."
—Alan Weiss, PhD, author, *Million Dollar Consulting* and *Thrive!*

Chicken Soup for the Christian Soul 2
Book and CD combo
The latest addition to the world-renowned Chicken Soup series, this book features Willie Jolley and Joyce Meyer on the front cover and includes a full-length CD of Willie Jolley's message "The Best Is Yet to Come." This incredible book and CD package contains stories of faith, hope, and healing.

"We are excited to announce that your story "They Got In!" was chosen to be included in our "101 Best Stories" books, representing readers all-time favorites from our library of stories." —The Chicken Soup for the Soul Team

Motivate Your Youth
(Dare 2 Dream/ Dare 2 Win) DVD
Willie Jolley is at his best in front of this packed audience of teenagers. He presents a powerful program on drug and alcohol prevention, violence prevention, academic excellence, and the need for making wise choices. Every home and school should have this DVD!

"I got my son to look at Willie Jolley's youth DVD after he decided to drop out of school. He was so motivated that he went back to school and finished. He even made the Honor Roll! What an awesome message!" —Tony Parker

The Speaking Success Package (T.I.P.S.)
Do you desire a career in public speaking? Do you believe you can motivate others to reach their full potential? Do you want help in achieving this goal? Willie Jolley shares how he went from being a no-name speaker to becoming Toastmasters International Speaker of the Year!

"WOW . . . I invested in Willie Jolley's Speaking Success Package and listened to the CD "How to Go From Unknown to Known in a Year," and it was magnificent! It provided superb information and inspiration. Plus I have immediately seen incredible growth in my speaking business." —Doreen Rainey, author and speaker

The Entrepreneurs Rich Success Treasure Chest
Millions of people want to become entrepreneurs but are not sure how  to accomplish it! In this package, Jolley shares his secrets for entrepreneurial success with people who want to grow and go to the next level in their personal and professional achievements! 5 CDs, 1 DVD, 1 workbook

"I started at the bottom of the company rankings. After listening to your CD's and putting into practice your knowledge and advice, I have made my way to the Top 5 in the company of 180 agents. While my colleagues are finding it tough in the "current real estate climate, I am working at it smarter, for better results." —John McManus, Sydney, Australia

Money Making Music and Motivation!
Do you want to make more money and have greater success? Do you commute to work? Use your commute time to grow your wealth! Make your car a rolling university! Ready to grow your future and your finances? The new Willie Jolley *Money Making Music and Motivation* collection will help you grow your faith, your future, and your finances! It contains 2 CDs, a full-length DVD, and a book, all in one package! It is dynamite!

"I listen to Willie Jolley's Motivational Music every day, and it has had a powerful impact on my business and my life! I highly recommend Willie Jolley's *Money Making Music* because . . . IT WORKS!" —Dr. Rena Vakay

WILLIE JOLLEY SPEAKING PROGRAMS

AN ATTITUDE OF EXCELLENCE

An Attitude of Excellence: 5 Simple Steps for 5 Star Success is Willie Jolley's answer to the age-old question: What secrets help 5 star organizations create consistent success? Willie's solutions have come from working with Fortune 500 corporations. This highly entertaining and comprehensive program is based on his work with these leading decision makers, spanning more than a decade!

"Your Attitude of Excellence message was the highest-rated program to date, and that is over six years. You hit the ball out of the park!"
—Al Cornish, vice president of learning for Norton Healthcare Systems

TURNING SETBACKS INTO COMEBACKS (AND GREENBACKS!)

Taken from Willie Jolley's popular book and PBS television special, *Turning Setbacks into Comebacks.* In this program, Willie Jolley explains how to come back from personal and professional setbacks and prosper! He shares tremendous techniques, ideas, principles, and strategies that others have used to go from being broke to being millionaires and from losing everything to creating super success stories!

"THANK YOU . . . not only for your inspiring message of hope and tenacity. YOU DESERVE TO BE LABELED ONE OF AMERICA'S VERY BEST SPEAKERS! You delivered!"
—Marty Reuter, president of Weichert Realtors

CHANGE IS GOOD ... WHEN YOUR ATTITUDE IS GREAT!

In this program, Willie Jolley shares how *all* progress is the result of change and through his patented "VDAD" (vision, decision, action, desire) formula for successfully embracing change. You will leave this program viewing change as an ally—not an enemy—and see that change truly is good ... when your attitude is great!

"I have received numerous compliments from attendees and will share their feedback with you once evaluations are completed. Great presentation. Great energy. Great mass appeal. Keep it up! We really appreciate Willie helping us kick off our New Year on a very positive and motivating start!"

HOW TO BE UNSTOPPABLE! LEADERSHIP AND ACHIEVEMENT!

Willie Jolley believes leadership is an action not a position! He reminds us that great leaders always focus on the possibilities rather than the challenges and are willing to do whatever is necessary rather than doing what is comfortable. Leaders look to develop more leaders rather than more followers!

Willie Jolley takes you on a memorable roller-coaster ride of why you must develop the leader within you and then gives you the steps for getting it done! It requires sweat equity, but so does anything of great achievement.

Whether you are an association executive, sales professional, entrepreneur, business owner, or manager, you will experience growth and renewed enthusiasm for reaching and exceeding your goals. This program will develop more leaders and set them on a course for becoming unstoppable!

THE JOLLEY INSTITUTE (PERSONAL AND PROFESSIONAL DEVELOPMENT SEMINARS)

The Jolley Institute addresses the varying needs of its clients by incorporating small-group structure, interactive training, and keynote presentations—all designed to help participants successfully apply the concepts, resources, and tools when they return to their respective workplaces!

Our approach to instruction is based on the premise that understanding the **"why"** of behavior and concepts makes the **"how"**—the practice and the implementation of new behavior and concepts—easier to internalize and implement!

The Institute believes that business and personal success is first the result of an attitude of excellence that says, "I can, and I will." That attitude of excellence translates into improved performance, improved communications, improved customer relations, and increased growth, which all focus on a commitment to bottom-line results!

Motivational Speaking 101
Learn how to start or grow your speaking business from "one of the top five speakers in the world"! Learn the secrets for rapidly growing your speaking business.

Presentation Skills
The greatest leaders are always excellent communicators. Studies show that most people have a fear of public speaking. This seminar helps alleviate that fear and develop the skills to become a professional speaker.

Jolley Relationship Seminar
Willie and Dee Jolley offer an exclusive retreat for couples who want to grow their relationships as they grow their businesses.

Entrepreneurs Boot Camp
Willie Jolley offers strategies for those who want to grow their entrepreneurial expertise and increase their net worth.

ACKNOWLEDGMENTS

I want to thank my wife, Dee Taylor-Jolley, for her efforts in keeping me focused so that this book would go from thought to reality; my marketing manager, Cheryl Ragin, for her efficiency in getting this manuscript ready for final print.

Thank you to all the people who served as readers and encouragers of this project. I especially want to thank Bill and Biddy Clark, Nina and Brian Taylor, Linda O'Doughda, and Carlene Reid for their honesty and editing; the members of my Mastermind Group, Bill Cates, Steven Gaffney, Suzi Pomerantz, and Zemira Jones for their frank feedback and subject-matter expertise; Jeff Kleinman, Wendy Keller, and Jeff Herman for their literary advice; Jeanette Boudreau and Elaine English for the wise legal counsel; and Ed Albert and his team at Flow Motion for their pre-publication versions of this book. To all my guests from my XM Radio Show and my friends at the National Speakers Association for their thoughts and advice, I am forever grateful. I appreciate you.

Thank you to Fred Johnson and Deacon Stanley Featherstone for helping me formulate the ideas for this book by asking me to help develop the "First Touch Leadership Professional

Development Program" at the First Baptist Church of Glenarden, Glenarden, MD; and all the churches and corporate groups who invited me to speak for their teams about "An Attitude of Excellence." Those sessions had a tremendous impact on helping me solidify the major points in the book.

A special thank you to Dr. Stephen Covey for his kindness and encouragement while I was finalizing the concepts in this book.

And all the wonderful folks at Greenleaf Book Group for their extraordinary work on getting this project completed with "an attitude of excellence"! And I want to say a special thank you to my friend Clint Greenleaf for his going above and beyond the call of duty in helping me get this book to print!

Last, but definitely not least, I want to thank my Friend and my Father, my Mentor and my Master, my Rock and my Redeemer, my Light and my Lord, my Source and my Savior—many regard Him as a simple carpenter from Galilee, but I consider Him to be my best friend! His name is Jesus! And I give Him glory for allowing me to write this book and see it to fruition.